Dialogues with Children and Adolescents

Psychoanalytic work with children is well-established and respected, but the sophisticated language used in psychoanalytic discourse can be at odds with how children communicate, and how best to communicate with them. *Dialogues with Children and Adolescents: A Psychoanalytic Guide* shows how these aims can be achieved for the most effective clinical outcome with children, from infancy up to late adolescence.

Björn Salomonsson and Majlis Winberg Salomonsson draw on extensive case material which reveals the essence of communication between child and therapist. They enfranchise the patient of all ages as an equal participant in the therapeutic relationship. Presented in letter form, the cases contain no professional terms. Only the final chapter contains theoretical commentaries applicable to each case. These terms and theories help to explain a child's behaviour, the analyst's technique and the background to the disorder.

This is new creative development in child therapy and analysis which is written in a very accessible style. *Dialogues with Children and Adolescents* will be essential reading for beginners in psychoanalytic work with children and will cast a fresh light on such work for more experienced clinicians. It will also appeal to the non-professional lay reader.

Björn Salomonsson is a Swedish psychoanalyst in private practice and at the Mama Mia Child Health Centre. He is also a researcher at the Department of Women's and Children's Health, Karolinska Institutet, Stockholm. He has published on containment, the analysis of children with ADHD, various subjects on infant-mother psychoanalysis and on case presentation methods. His book *Psychoanalytic Therapy with Infants and Parents* was published by Routledge in 2014.

Majlis Winberg Salomonsson is a Swedish training and child psychoanalyst. She works in private practice and is a lecturer at the Faculty of Psychology, University of Stockholm. Majlis is also a researcher at the Department of Women's and Children's Health, Karolinska Institutet, Stockholm. She has published papers on psychoanalysis with children and adolescents.

Dialogues with Children and Adolescents

A Psychoanalytic Guide

Björn Salomonsson and
Majlis Winberg Salomonsson

LONDON AND NEW YORK

First published in English in 2016 as *Dialogues with Children and Adolescents: A Psychoanalytic Guide*

by Routledge
2 Park Square, Milton Park, Abingdon, Oxon OX14 4RN

and by Routledge
711 Third Avenue, New York, NY 10017

Routledge is an imprint of the Taylor & Francis Group, an informa business

© 2016 Björn Salomonsson and Majlis Winberg Salomonsson

The right of Björn Salomonsson and Majlis Winberg Salomonsson to be identified as authors of this work has been asserted by them in accordance with sections 77 and 78 of the Copyright, Designs and Patents Act 1988.

This work is a translation of a work previously published in Swedish as: *Brev från barnens O* 2012

by Carlssons Bokförlag
Translation into English by Pamela Boston

All rights reserved. No part of this book may be reprinted or reproduced or utilised in any form or by any electronic, mechanical, or other means, now known or hereafter invented, including photocopying and recording, or in any information storage or retrieval system, without permission in writing from the publishers.

Trademark notice: Product or corporate names may be trademarks or registered trademarks, and are used only for identification and explanation without intent to infringe.

British Library Cataloguing in Publication Data
A catalogue record for this book is available from the British Library

Library of Congress Cataloging-in-Publication Data
Salomonsson, Björn, author.
  [Brev från barnens O. English]
  Dialogues with children and adolescents : a psychoanalytic guide / Bjorn Salomonsson and Majlis Winberg Salomonsson.
    pages cm
  "This work is a translation of a work previously published in Swedish as: Brev från barnens O 2012."
  1. Child analysis. 2. Child psychotherapy. 3. Parent and child. I. Salomonsson, Majlis Winberg, author. II. Title.
  RJ504.2.S24713 2016
  618.92'8914—dc23
  2015031372

ISBN: 978-1-138-88464-9 (hbk)
ISBN: 978-1-138-88465-6 (pbk)
ISBN: 978-1-315-71596-4 (ebk)

Typeset in Times
by Apex CoVantage, LLC

Contents

Introduction   1

1. The Land of O   6
2. The hole in the escalator   11
3. Why are they doing like that?   19
4. Raging with love   27
5. Here comes Pippi Lundström   35
6. You'll be deader than dead   43
7. We don't look into each other's eyes   49
8. My head is a mess   53
9. Restless and ruthless – or just rootless?   59
10. Letter from the volcano   66
11. That tingling feeling   75
12. No connection   79
13. The first time that I saw you   86

14	The last time that I saw you	100
15	Commentaries on Chapters 2–12	113
	References	147
	Index	153

Introduction

"Anyone who has travelled has a story to tell". Or, as the old saying figured in our secondary school German grammar books, "*Wer eine Reise tut, hat etwas zu erzählen*". We are two psychoanalysts who have "travelled" a great deal with children and youngsters. However, we are not referring to tourist trips to faraway places or countries. Rather, our journeys have always had the same destination – our consulting rooms. Our itineraries may have seemed monotonous, at least in the external sense of the word; every meeting took place in the same office room, with the same analyst. However, a closer look reveals the itineraries to have been varied and unpredictable; we encountered children who were crying in despair, giggling in excitement, roaring with anger and telling us horror stories with Dickensian imagination.

As the years went by, we felt an increasing need to tell others about our experiences. We started to write a kind of travel book, portraying the feelings and thoughts of children and youngsters. Young people sometimes leave us completely out in the cold by something they do or say. At other times they impress us as being incredibly funny and inventive. They may even go as far as to seem infinitively complicated or enigmatic. Indeed, they themselves are often unaware of why they are doing all these things. No wonder children often seem incomprehensible to us adults. We hesitate to give our readers a little language lesson at this stage, but we just have to! In Swedish, our mother tongue, many words that are used to make negations begin with the prefix "o". For example, "intressant" means interesting and "ointressant" means uninteresting. Children, however, never appear "O-interesting" to us. They rather strike us as "O-believable", "O-imaginable", "O-comprehensible", and "O-predictable". In the end we concluded that our impressions of the children we had met over the years could be summarized into one single letter: O!

At this stage of our discussions, the "Land of O" emerged as an apt metaphor of the child's inner world. How were we to visualize this "land" to readers who perhaps had not been as close to it as we had? Our solution was to do the same thing as we ourselves did when we were travelling youths: to write a set of "letters from the Land of O", back and forth between the children and ourselves. In fact, we had yet another reason to choose the letter O. However, let us not jump ahead without first addressing a question that you as a reader must certainly be posing already: "For whom is this book written?"

Our book addresses anyone who has been puzzled about a little child's strange remarks, the funny hobbies of a young school child or a teenager's contradictory emotions. Perhaps you are a grandfather or a grandmother, or maybe a parent, who is concerned about what might be troubling your grandchild or child. Alternatively, you might be young yourself and wonder about your own feelings and actions as well as those of young people around you. Or you might be a professional working with children at a preschool, a school, an after-school or hobby programme or within a health care facility. Sooner or later, everyone who spends time with a child will end up asking why they seem so "O-comprehensible". Indeed, most of us have tried to understand – most often in vain – what lies behind the desperate crying of the little baby, the obstinate sulking of the two-year-old, the agitated troublemaking of the six-year-old or the endless emotional swings of the fifteen-year-old.

As psychoanalysts, we work with children in a way that enables us to get to know each one of them individually through lengthy dialogues in a relationship – and quite an intense one at that. Together with the child, we have been swept into the midst of many stormy emotions. After hard work, together with the child in psychotherapy, we have been able to get out of these storms and have thus come to understand them better. We have found out something about the depths of the child. Such recesses are not easy to access when you see a child more sporadically or in a less focused situation. As we see it, one of the best places for discovering them is the psychotherapist's office. One major aim of the book is therefore to provide examples from our daily practice of what a child may look like internally.

When we explain that our stories are presented in the form of a correspondence between the children and us, please do not misunderstand us. In Chapter 2, our first letter-writer, "Bonnie", is two and a half years old. She obviously did not write what you will read there. Her letters, like those of the other children, are rather our way of conveying how we think children and youngsters feel inside. We refer to how they think and feel, what they contemplate and what makes them so overwhelmed by things that we adults think are mere trivialities. Some letters refer to various dialogues and events that have taken place during therapy. Does this mean that we write letters to our patients in reality? No, the letters are our mode of clarifying and bringing out what has been going on in our consulting rooms. In this way, we are able to provide the perspectives of both parties, the children and ourselves. As you will see, not every letter-writer in the book is based upon a patient whom we have actually met. Some are literary persons whom we have chosen in order to illustrate issues which many children are struggling with today.

Any therapist who wants to write about patients meets with the task of protecting their anonymity. As for our young patients, such as Maya, Noah and other children in the book, their stories have been de-identified and they have been given other names. Every time we felt the least hesitation, we consulted the parents to get their approval for publication. As for Pippi Longstocking (or Hanna Lundström, as we name a girl who identifies strongly with Pippi), Ronia, the robber's daughter, and Moses from the Bible, the stories represent our fantasies about these famous characters. We hope they will not mind our rummaging about a little with their lives . . .

Every chapter can also be read from a theoretical perspective. Theory – we know that word sounds thorny and difficult! However, the truth is that every human being regards the world and his fellow human beings from theoretical perspectives. We do not always make these theories clear to ourselves. Nevertheless, they are there and they influence us. You may have said something like, "My goodness, Charlie is really a pain but after all he's going through his terrible twos." Or, "My boss just got divorced. I guess he's having a typical midlife crisis." These statements are actually based on your theories about why people behave as they do, regardless of whether they are toddlers or middle-aged men.

Our stories have been written from a psychoanalytic perspective. Similarly to the more commonplace theories like the ones mentioned earlier, psychoanalysis also has things to say about troublemaking Charlie and your newly divorced boss, as well as many other emotional phenomena seen in human beings. However, it does so much more systematically and comprehensively. Many people tend to distance themselves from terms like "the Unconscious" or "the Oedipus complex". They might feel reverence or even awe and claim that these terms are too exclusive and incomprehensible for them to use at all. Or, they might be sceptical and assert that modern science has proved the theories behind the terms to be obsolete, false or not evidence-based. To us, psychoanalytic theory is simply a smart way of describing what goes on when we meet our patients in our consulting rooms – as well as when we meet a child in the playground who is making trouble or a boss at the office who is having a midlife crisis. We hope to show you that psychoanalytic theory is neither too exclusive to be used by laymen nor too obsolete to be used by us, people of the twenty-first century.

Theories are like the headlights on the runway at an airport. Without them no airplane would be able to land. Similarly, without theories no human being is able to think. This airplane metaphor was once suggested by an Israeli colleague, Abigail Golomb. Well, in your daily life you do not tend to think about "anal fixations" or "unresolved Oedipal ties to the mother" when you want to explain little Charlie's outbursts or the midlife crisis of your boss! Psychoanalytic theories are more complicated than the everyday theories we all use when we get bewildered. This divergence between commonplace theories and psychoanalytic conceptualisations became an issue for us when we were writing the book. How could we render "our" theory vital and accessible?

Here is our way of solving the theory issue: Chapters 2–14, where children and their difficulties are presented mainly through letters, are written without any professional terms whatsoever. Nevertheless, for each child portrayed, some theoretical perspectives are especially relevant. In the conclusive chapter of the book, Chapter 15, we bring out and clarify these perspectives. Here, we use psychoanalytic terms to comment on each case, regardless of whether it involves a clinical or a literary child. A psychotherapist will thus recognize herself or himself in reading the final chapter. If he or she is working with children, he or she might also find the book useful to explain to parents and teachers what psychotherapy for young people is all about and what it can achieve. In addition, we often meet many non-professionals who think that psychology is interesting and who wonder what these terms actually imply. If you are interested in the child's inner world and in how we can help youngsters deal with their issues, you can get into your studious mood and read our travellers' stories and the commentaries as an introduction to child psychotherapy. If your mood is more laid-back you can just read the correspondences and browse through the conclusive theoretical chapter. We would like to thank editor Maija Zeile Westrup for giving us the idea of adding the final theoretical chapter. We also extend our warm thanks to Pamela Boston, who translated the book from Swedish and provided many valuable suggestions.

It is about time to start our travel reports, but before you decide to come along with us, you naturally wish to know who we are. Both of us are psychoanalysts in private practice, and we also teach and supervise at the Swedish Psychoanalytic Institute in Stockholm, including its Reception Service for Child Psychoanalysis. Our patients are children, youngsters and adults. Björn is a psychiatrist and a consultant psychoanalyst at the Mama Mia Child Health Centre in Stockholm. Majlis is a psychologist and child psychotherapist trained at the Erica Foundation in Stockholm, where she is also a teacher. Björn's academic dissertation project was a randomized controlled trial (RCT) of mother-infant psychoanalytic treatment. The project issued from the Division of Child Psychiatry, the Department of Women's and Children's Health, Karolinska Institutet, Stockholm. The two of us are now pursuing a follow-up study on the children, who have reached four and a half years of age. At the time of this book's publication, the results will be published in the Infant Mental Health Journal.

Björn has published papers on child psychoanalysis and two monographs. One is in Swedish and deals with psychoanalytic consultations with parents and infants at a child health centre. The other is in English: "Psychoanalytic Therapy with Infants and Parents: Practice, theory and results" (Salomonsson, 2014). Majlis has published papers on child analysis and, together with Björn Wrangsjö, a Swedish textbook on adolescent development and psychotherapy.

Now you know who we are and what we want to achieve with this book. Come along with us to the "O-comprehensible", "O-predictable" and "O-imaginable" inner world of children and youngsters, a place also known as "the Land of O"!

Chapter 1

The Land of O

The Land of O can be described as a faraway place, which we have discovered through our psychoanalytic dialogues with children and youngsters. We have already described some of its characteristics: strange, crazy, moving, funny, illogical or just puzzling. Once one embarks on a journey to the Land of O, questions emerge effortlessly: Why does the baby in his pram suddenly start to scream? Why do we witness such a storm of protest from a three-year-old who knows that his waterproof trousers are comfortable in the rain but who nevertheless refuses to put them on? Why do we hear incessant giggling from the ten-year-old girls in the school restroom? And what about the exchange of glances among the fourteen-year-olds when the teacher is strolling across the schoolyard?

In therapy with children, the questions are similar but more complicated. Let us give an example: six-year-old Anthony, whom we will meet in Chapters 13 and 14, is trying in vain to understand why he is so stressed and worried. His family goes on a holiday trip. When he returns to his therapist he says, "We had a great time in England. We took a boat there. You can do that you know – you don't have to fly. The boat even carried our car and a lot of trucks, too. But before we left, I got the traveller's fever. Mum explained it to me when I couldn't fall asleep; it was the night before we started our trip." He thinks for a while and suddenly bursts out excitedly, "Now I know what I've got. I've got the traveller's fever! I've got it all the time, and you see what happens. I just can't sit still on my chair." Anthony is a hyperactive boy having a hard time focusing on his tasks at school. Now he is describing how he was eagerly and anxiously waiting for the family trip. Suddenly he realizes that he is also describing how he may get anxious in other instances without understanding why. Thanks to his new application of the term "traveller's fever", his constant anxiety becomes a little more manageable than before.

Another instance is a teenager's parent who is met with a cascade of angry outbursts from his or her child, "You damned idiot! You never let me do what I want to do and one day, I bet, you won't even let me leave home and you're worse than a dictator and you . . . !" Catherine rushes into her room. After a while she phones her best friend and has a chat with her for one hour at least. We overhear her saying that a certain boy who has filled her heart and mind for the last few months has recently been treating her badly. In such moments, the incomprehensibility of her angry cascade melts away and we are able to look into some of the innermost feelings concealed beneath it.

Many times a child may seem beyond understanding because we adults try to persuade ourselves that we are so different from our little ones. But actually, we carry the same kinds of emotions that they do even though we handle them in different ways. Let us illustrate: Uno is one year old and he has just learnt to walk. He is immensely proud. But every time he loses his balance and tumbles down, he cries for Mum. She gives him a mug of lemonade but he throws it on the floor. He is in despair and is also ashamed and angry. Falling down on the floor was a catastrophe. After a while he looks at the lemonade, has a sip and shines up. Out of the blue, he forgets everything and starts walking happily again. At this precise moment his mother is thinking about Uno's grandparent, her father. Towards the end of his life, old Sidney has become paralyzed and now spends his days in a wheelchair. Sid, who used to be quite a sociable fellow, nowadays accepts only occasional visits from his family or friends. He has become depressed because he feels that he has turned into a "vegetable rotting at a retirement home", as he describes himself. Last week Sid called his daughter to tell her about his dream the night before. "Without any problem whatsoever, I was flying about in the sky, visiting all my children and grandchildren. It didn't matter much that they are living all around the world! No paralysis any longer and no depression either – at least for the time being."

Old Sid and young Uno are both struggling with the pain of having lost an ability they thought they had mastered: the ability to walk. The pain and the paralysis "get on my psyche", as Sid explained to his daughter, but he and his grandson Uno react to this pain in different ways. The following night Sid dreamt that he had been fettered with a heavy chain to a rock. That dream was not as pleasant as the one preceding it. "I guess that's the way I feel, like Prometheus bound to the rock. I suppose some eagles will come soon and pick me up for good." Things do not look that way for young Uno. His desperate feelings of some seconds ago are soon forgotten. This is a fellow who lives in the present moment! The next time he falls on the ground he gets up quickly and runs along. Until he falls again . . .

In the introduction, we suggested that we had more reasons for introducing the letter O when describing the world of children. We also use the circular letter O to represent the infinity of the child's inner world:

Unendlich in German, *Oändlig* in Swedish. People often grant that children and adults do have the same kinds of feelings. Nevertheless, they are convinced that children's feelings cannot really be as complicated as those of adults, at least not complicated enough to lead to some of the behaviour they see. So they turn to us, asking, "You are a child therapist. Could you please explain why this child is constantly quarrelling?" The one seeking an explanation may be a parent in a difficult situation at home or a teacher who cannot come to terms with a troublemaker in the classroom. Here is an example of what an adult might tell us: "Every time I talk to Adrian, and I am quite friendly to him, he snaps back, 'Oh, won't you just shut up!' It's terrible to hear and I just can't stand it! Tell me, what's wrong with him?"

Of course, it is provocative and painful to hear words like these from another human being, regardless of his or her age. But people who want a quick explanation for such behaviour often assume that mental life is simpler and more understandable in children than in adults. This is not the case, according to our experience. We often have to answer, "You have just asked a difficult question. I will answer you to the best of my ability, but please do not expect any simple response or quick solutions." The mental world of the child is as infinite and complicated as that of the adult. It is replete with creative but maybe far-fetched notions, crazy misunderstandings, wild leaps of emotion, morality debates, raging love affairs, passionate hatred, shrewd schemes and artistic conceptions. And for a description of the adolescent's turmoil we find no better one than Anna Freud's (1958), which was written half a century ago. She describes,

> the anxieties, the height of elation or depth of despair, the quickly rising enthusiasms, the utter hopelessness, the burning – or at other times sterile – intellectual and philosophical preoccupations, the yearning for freedom, the sense of loneliness, the feeling of oppression by the parents, the impotent rages or active hates directed against the adult world, the erotic crushes – whether homosexually or heterosexually directed – the suicidal fantasies, etc.
>
> (P. 260)

The Land of O is thus *Oändligt* or infinite. Our letter O also relates to the term the Unconscious: *das Unbewußte* in German, *det Omedvetna* in Swedish. We would like to explain that term in the following way: when we are working intensively with a child, we observe everything she or he says, draws, plays and dreams. We imagine ourselves as standing outside the child's O. In this respect, we are like anyone else in front of a child. But we do something more: we try to imagine what is going on inside the ring of the O – that is, in his/her Unconscious. This latter term is not easy to grasp. You cannot put your finger on the Unconscious; you cannot make a blood test to measure it, or take a picture of it in a scanner or with an X-ray. None of us ever seems to be quite comfortable with the fact that we cannot reach these remote corners within ourselves – that is, all our contradictory fantasies, feelings and memories. The Swedish poet Gunnar Ekelöf (1965, p. 144) once expressed it this way: "Every human being is a world, inhabited by blind beings in dark revolt against the I, the King, their master."

We see and are blind – both at the same time. The Conscious is perhaps not so difficult to describe. But how are we to acknowledge and describe all those thoughts and feelings we knew yesterday but do not remember today, or those we have never quite understood but which nevertheless affect us throughout our lives? We provide a tentative answer via a poetic metaphor by the French author Albert Camus (1994). He compares the unconscious layers of our personality to "those measureless waters under the earth which . . . have never seen the light of day and yet dimly reflect a light, come from who knows where" (p. 278). Not only are these subterranean layers vast and difficult to fathom. In addition it is only hesitantly that we set out to uncovering them, and the more we approach them the more we tend to close our eyes. It is no wonder that the Delphic Maxim γνῶθι σεαυτόν (*gnothi seauton* or "know thyself") is so hard to live by. This also applies to children. They often seem spontaneous and uninhibited, but they, too, have internal recesses that they shun and prefer not to know more about.

So far, we have brought in sources from Sweden, ancient Greece and France to portray the internal world of children, or, as we call it, the Land of O. It is time to bring in a source from another country, the English psychoanalyst W.R. Bion (1970). He used the letter O to denote "ultimate reality, absolute truth, the godhead, the infinite, the thing-in-itself" (p. 26) of our inner world. A renowned scholar in this field, the US psychoanalyst James Grotstein (2008), emphasizes that Bion saw the mind as unfathomable and infinite, and that it depended on the therapist's so-called negative capability, or his or her tolerance of uncertainty and ambiguity, if he or she could wait outside of O to capture whatever signals might be emitted.

We prefer to compare the relationship between O and the external world – with all its sense impressions and observations – to a permeable cell membrane. There is ceaseless traffic of information passing from the Unconscious, the "measureless waters" or "the Land of O", through the membrane to reach the person standing outside. As analysts we are waiting outside the child's "membrane", and we try to understand the signals to the best of our ability. Sometimes instantly and spontaneously, sometimes only upon lengthy reflection, we may suggest to the child what we envisage he or she is trying to express or is preoccupied with. Only rarely does a child, especially someone who is having emotional difficulties, understand why he or she is jumping about all the time, has nightmares or refuses to put on waterproof trousers when it is time to go to preschool. Nor does he usually understand the origin of his funny ideas and fantastic drawings. "It just came out that way!" Similarly to an adult, a child has an unconscious world which has never seen "the light of day" but which nevertheless is emitting signals across the "cell membrane". These are the signals that we as analysts try to decipher in order to help the child. In doing this, we contribute to making the dim reflection clearer to him. In these circumstances, he may become able to find words for what has been frightening him, as in the case of young Anthony when he said, "Aha, I've got the traveller's fever!" It was as if this expression opened up a shaft to his "O". With its help he was now able to better discern what was troubling him, and to express this in words.

Does our cell membrane model imply that the analyst also has unconscious inner notions? Is he or she also an inhabitant of the Land of O? Definitively! Here is our argument: no one would be surprised to learn that curiosity is vital for a psychotherapist. Furthermore, he or she must be persistent and systematic, intuitive and courageous, and must not shy away from embarrassing facts and unpleasant findings. After all, such a relentless and compassionate search for the truth goes for anybody pursuing a scientific effort or, for that matter, anyone wanting to get close to another human being, be it a partner, a friend or a patient in a dialogue. But the psychoanalyst needs another asset as well, that of turning curiosity towards *him/herself* in order to ask why he or she reacts this or that way with a patient: "Why did I become so moved by this boy right now?" Or: "Why do I find this girl to be so charming at today's session?" This procedure, when the analyst explores his own personal Land of O, is defined as making use of the countertransference. We use this term to cover the emotional reactions, not least the unconscious ones, of the analyst vis-à-vis the patient. By investigating his or her reactions, the analyst may better understand what is going on inside the patient. Does this sound complicated? We hope it will become clearer as you go along reading the book! Let us go to the letter box and open the first letter.

Chapter 2

The hole in the escalator

Hi there, Björn!
Here's a letter from someone who visits you at your office and who's two and a half years old. Aha, you guessed it! Bonnie! Mummy often says that I'm her little sweetie pie. Of course, I like that – but at the same time I don't like it. I'm sure you understand. Sometimes when I hear it I start to sulk. That's because I like to think of myself as a cool kid who can be tough and fight for her own way if she wants to. And I can put up a big fuss! But of course I don't do it all the time.

But never mind all that. I'm writing because I want to tell you something: one day, Mum and I were going somewhere on the underground. I like to ride the underground very much. The wheels of the train screech and click and make all kinds of funny noises. And there are so many kinds of people inside. Yes, even dogs sometimes! The little ones sit in their owners' laps. That's cute. I don't get as afraid as when I see the bigger dogs standing by the exit door. But this thing I want to tell you about now, it happened outside the train, after we had left it.

I've been to this underground station many times before but this time, everything was different. When we were about to step onto the escalator, it was gone and, instead, there was a big hole! The escalator wasn't where it used to be. I saw a lot of men with some hard hats on their heads. They were working there, I reckon! Mummy told me they were going to fix the escalator because it was broken. They had taken it away and now there were machines instead. There was a huge clanking noise so I got really scared and then that big hole, too! I mean the hole where the escalator had been all the other times when I was there with Mum.

I started to cry. Mum took me up into her arms and told me we were going to take the elevator instead. She thought it was the elevator's fault that I got scared! No, it was the *hole* that was so terrible. I can't explain why. Mum asked me if I was afraid of falling down into it. Maybe. I didn't know. When I went to bed that night I couldn't go to sleep. Wherever I looked I thought I saw that hole right there gaping at me.

I cried for Mum. She sounded a little annoyed when she answered me. She tends to sound that way when I call out for her. I think it's because I do that quite often when I'm having a hard time falling asleep. Well, I have to admit I call out for her for many other reasons as well, like when I want some extra toothpaste on my toothbrush because it tastes so good – or when I don't want to put on my red T-shirt because it's so ugly. Mum and Dad don't understand why I care about stuff like that, and they say I'm being bossy and picky.

Yes, they say I cry out too much and that I make trouble for them. Well, maybe so. But the thing is that I'm frightened! It's like when there was that ghost who dreamt me, just about when I was going to sleep. Then I ran to Mum and Dad, to sleep in their bed. Daddy said, "Oh, no! Not again!" He turned over and fell asleep. Mum said, "Okay, but only this time." So, she let me sleep next to her. The next morning they seemed to be annoyed with me and, would you believe it, with each other as well! When Daddy spilled some marmalade on his trousers, he looked angrily at Mum and said that it was because of the bad night's sleep he got. Then they both looked at me. Those looks didn't feel good.

Ugh! Ghosts and that hole in the escalator. No, I don't want to think about these things anymore, I really don't. And you know what? I don't have time to tell you any more right now. I'm going out to play with Neda. She has just moved into our neighbourhood. She comes from another country and has a funny way of speaking. She's nice. I think we can be friends.

So long and have a nice day,

Bonnie

Response from Björn

Hello Bonnie!

Thanks for your letter. Here is a letter from me. I'm writing to you from Copenhagen. I've just visited a museum there. A museum is a big house where you can look at many paintings and statues. There is an awesome statue here and when I saw it, I instantly thought of you. I am sending you a photo of it. The man who made it is called Christian Lemmerz.

Of course, this statue does not look like you at all. You are a lovely girl with curly hair and brown eyes, nothing like this statue. Why did I think of you? Well, I was thinking about that hole in the escalator that you were telling me about in your letter. Can you see that the statue doesn't have any face and has a big black hole instead? The escalator hole and the hole in the statue remind me of when you were at my office and you mentioned a hole that you thought was so scary. Wow, how many times did we talk about that hole after that!? At least a hundred times before you became a little less scared!

Perhaps you think the escalator hole has got nothing to do with the statue. After all, they don't look alike at all! You might be right there. But then I thought about how you like to play with the big armchair in my consulting room. One day, you discovered that if you took the cushion off of that armchair, there was just the wooden frame left. This frame has got a big hole in it. As soon as you discovered it, you wanted to crawl through the hole over and over again. Then something occurred to me. The statue and my armchair, each of them has a big hole that maybe is frightening to you, just like you say the escalator hole is. I wonder what

that could mean. If you happen to think of an answer you can write it down in a letter to me.

All the best,

Björn

My ghost drawings – response from Bonnie

Hi again Björn!

Yes, I remember something that might help explain that hole stuff. It might be the ghosts. You remember how I used to be so frightened of them. I was a bit younger than today. At the beginning I didn't know what the ghosts looked like. I just knew they were there when I was about to fall asleep. Then I told Mum about them, but she said that ghosts

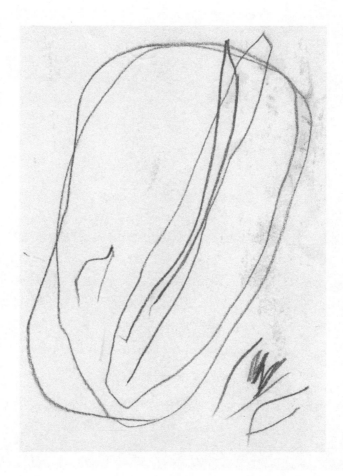

don't exist. I didn't believe her because I *knew* they were there. When I told you about them you asked me what they looked like. I made my first ghost drawing and showed it to you.

You looked a bit puzzled when you took a look at my drawing. I guess it was because you didn't grasp what it meant. Neither did I! After all, I had never dared to look at the ghosts that were around me when I was trying to sleep. Later, when you and I started to talk about them, I began to be able to draw them a little bit better.

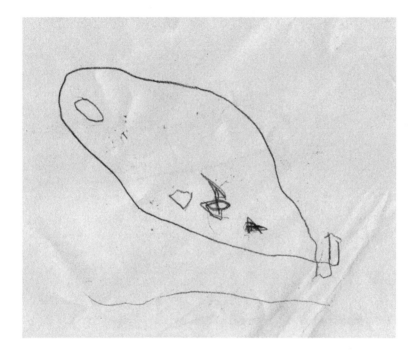

You were wondering why the mouth looked so small. "Of course, it should look like that," I told you. "It's not even a mouth! Don't you know that ghosts don't have any mouths?" No, you didn't seem to know anything about stuff like that. So I made another drawing to help you understand. As you can see for yourself, I crossed the mouth over with my pencil.

You asked me why ghosts don't have any mouths. "Don't you know? I guess you really don't know," I said. "It's because they can eat you." You told me that if they don't have mouths, they can't eat anything. Then I had to tell you, "Björn, you just don't understand. They eat you with the mouth they don't have." That's what makes these creatures so nasty!

16 The hole in the escalator

I really hope you understand me a little better now because it's time for me to leave for preschool!
So long for now,

Bonnie

The mum-hole – response from Björn

Hello Bonnie!
    I'm still in Copenhagen. I just had to go back to the museum in the morning and check on the statue without a face. It really puzzled me. Yesterday on the bus I saw a lady who reminded me a little of this statue. She had a head scarf around her face and did not look happy. I suddenly came to think of your mother. An idea struck me and that's what made me feel that I had to go back and check on that statue again. After I had done so, I left the museum thinking to myself, "Here I am in Copenhagen pondering on three ladies. The lady on the bus, the lady of the statue, and then Bonnie's mother. What is it about all three of them that puzzles me? They don't look alike at all!" But then I had another idea . . .
    When you were a tiny baby, your mother was quite sad. She told me and you about it when we worked together in my office. She was very

happy when you were born, but after that she started worrying that she was not a good mother. As soon as you would whimper the least little bit, she would think it was her fault. Nobody understood how sad she was or why she was so sad. I don't think she knew the reason herself. Was it because of you? Well, when you were a tiny baby, perhaps you kept thinking you could not reach out to her and so you looked away from her. Things are different today. Now you look right into people's eyes when you speak to them and should anyone neglect to look into your eyes, you surely let them know about it! But for a little baby, it is not so easy to look at her mother if she does not look back. When she is sad, she doesn't look very much at her baby. Perhaps your mother looked like this sad lady I saw on the bus. I got the impression that she was keeping "herself inside herself", if I may put it that way.

So I'm wondering if you were afraid already when you were a tiny baby. There are grown-ups who think babies can't be afraid. Well, I think they can. I think you got scared when you looked into your mother's eyes. It was as if you couldn't reach her all the way through, even while she was right in front of you. Perhaps that's when you got scared of holes. We might say that the first holes you were frightened of were your mother's sad eyes. But you couldn't tell her about it. After all, you can't speak about such things when you're a baby. Instead you turned into "quite a fussy girl", as your parents sometimes called you – even though they loved you very much.

Nowadays, you know how scared you've been, not only of the holes in the escalator and in my armchair, but also of the sad "Mum-holes" as we called them, you and I. Even a ghost's mouth became a nasty hole that did not exist but that could swallow you anyway! You are braver today. I think it's because you and I have talked through the things that have been so terrifying to you. The other day you told me you'd been able to sleep all through the night. You sounded very proud.

We will talk about all these things when we meet next time. I'll check on that statue once again at the museum. Then I'll take the night train back to Stockholm. That's great fun. Should a ghost appear on the train, I'll give him your greetings and tell him he can go to sleep somewhere else.

Björn

An e-mail from her mother some years after Bonnie ended therapy with Björn

Dear Björn!

Just a few lines. Three years have passed since Bonnie ended her treatment with you. Today she is six years old and robust in every way. She is a girl who is on the go and she has a lively temperament. Sometimes she can be taxing when she insists on getting things her way. But she sleeps well and she is not afraid any more. And when our wills clash, we are usually able to come to a solution. That's a big relief!

The other day, something remarkable happened. We were sitting at the breakfast table. Bonnie was having her cornflakes and milk as usual. All of a sudden she said, "Do you know Mum, it's funny but when I was little I was so frightened by the hole in the underground escalator. How weird!"

She didn't add anything more. Of course, I understood what she was referring to since I was there in the underground station when it happened. I asked her to tell me more, but she just shook her head, laughing and saying, "How crazy!" Then it was time to go to school. Yes, time passes quickly and Bonnie has just started school.

When Bonnie made this remark at the breakfast table, I thought of you and wanted you to know about it. After all, you were a passenger too on our journey. Those days, when we used to meet together, all three of us, you understood that I had been deep down in the doldrums. We could really say that I, as well as Bonnie, had been down in a kind of hole. It feels wonderful to be able to breathe more freely nowadays.

Best regards,

Nadia

Chapter 3

Why are they doing like that?

> "'You were in the woods a long time today,' Matt said as Ronia sat down by the fire to get warm. 'How was everything out there?' 'Not bad,' Ronia said as she held her ice-cold hands up to the fire."

Mummy had just finished reading to me from the book *Ronia, The Robber's Daughter*. She read the chapter where Ronia falls in the snow while she is skiing in the forest. One of her feet gets stuck in a trolls' hole, the kind of trolls that live in the underworld – or at least under the moss. I like it very much when Mother reads stories to me. Sometimes she can sound funny, though. She comes from Italy and there they don't have that letter "T". Well, they have it but it sounds more like our letter "D" because of the soft way they say it. So when Mum read the word "trolls", she pronounced it "drolls". That sounded so funny and made me laugh. Mum didn't understand why. I told her to pronounce it "trolls". I also told her that drolls sounded like "drool" and then I let some saliva drip out of the corner of my mouth and made a big bubble out of it. She got embarrassed and told me it was time to go to bed or as she put it, "Dime do go do bed, Peder." Well, okay, now I am exaggerating a bit, to tell you the truth. Then I got my goodnight kiss and she turned the light off and left the room.

I lay there in my bed in the dark. Since last summer, I've been able to sleep without a night light in my bedroom. I think it's pretty good for a chap of five years, if I may say so myself. I was thinking about the trolls in Ronia's story. Why did they keep asking themselves all the time, "Why is she doing like that?" They mean Ronia. Actually, they talk like this: "Whyffor did un do that?"

How silly they were! They didn't grasp anything at all. Like they didn't understand why Ronia was shaking her foot. Of course, it was because she was trying to get it out of the hole in the ground! She couldn't know that her foot had broken their roof. And they wondered why she was crying. Well, that was because she was sad to be trapped and she was afraid she might die all alone in the forest. At first, I thought the trolls were stupid but then I started thinking. There are many things I don't understand myself. I would really like to ask someone about them, "Why are you doing like that?"

Here's one thing I think about lots and lots: What happens when Mum says goodnight, leaves my room and closes the door? She often says, "I'm just going to tuck the little one into bed." Why does she do like that? I mean she already tucked him in once before she came to my room so why does she have to go back to him? My little brother is almost a year old. If he had been crying and whining at that moment – which he does all the time in the day but not at night – then I'd understand why she needs to tuck him to bed again. But she says that thing every night! And then she sounds different, a little nicer and sweeter. I heard her calling him "Caro". What does she mean by calling him that? It sounds like she's talking about a car! Sometimes I get a sting inside when she speaks that way. I think she loves my little brother more than she loves me. So why does she do like that?

Here's another thing that's even stranger: sometimes Daddy gives Mummy a hug. Okay, there's nothing weird about that. But they hug in different ways! When Dad comes home from work, he just gives her a quick hug and he looks very tired. But on Saturday night when we've been watching TV, he holds her tighter and says, "Darling, don't you think it's about time to put the children to bed? Let me take care of bedtime and you can just sit here and loosen up." Okay, most of the time my dad's friendly to her and to me as well. But that voice to Mum on Saturday night is superfriendly. And by the way, what does he mean by "loosen up"? I don't know but it sounds kind of cool.

I asked Charlie about this hugging stuff the other day. He's my best friend at preschool. He answered, "Oh, come on, Peter! Don't you understand why they're hugging? They're fucking!" I stopped Charlie right there and told him to shut up. My mum and dad don't do such things. I'm dead sure about that. I'll tell you how I know. I checked it out. Once I woke up in the middle of the night because I had a nasty dream. I got up, went to the loo and then sneaked into their bedroom. I saw them and heard them right up close. They were lying there snoring. They didn't even notice when I slipped into their bed and lay down between them. They were not doing what Charlie said. I'm positive about it, so Charlie was dead wrong when he said that.

But I don't really know what fuck means. So maybe I'm wrong. Maybe they did it another time. I know it has something to do with a dad's willie and that place where babies come out of a mom, out of a mom's, you know, eh, body. They told us about all that stuff at preschool. They also told us that adults feel good when they do it. What do they mean when they say it feels good? I just got a new bed cover, which I think feels very good. But maybe the thing Mum and Dad do feels good in another way? I sure have a lot of things to think about here: what my parents are doing, and why Mum is tucking my little brother into bed all the time. These are difficult questions and I haven't found any good answers – so far! One thing I have found out, though; I feel this sting inside every time I think about them.

You know what? I've figured out a way to get rid of that sting. I wind myself up! It's like those clown or monkey toys that you wind up and then they start jumping about. I shake my legs a little in bed, and then I start shaking my head as well. Then, I fling my entire body up and down and finally I jump on the bed. At last, the sting thing inside goes away! Of course, Mum returns to my room when she hears me jumping around. She says, "Stop that right now, Peter, and don't do it again!" But I want to go on doing it, because the sting goes away and she comes back to me. The other day I wound myself up full force. Of course, Mum came back to my room and then I said to her, "Now that you're back in my room, could you please read me another chapter about Ronia?" I thought she'd like the way I was being so polite and using the word "please". But I was dead wrong! She stomped about and looked really angry. In fact, she was so angry that I got scared, turned round and fell asleep on the spot. Anyway, I still wonder why she keeps tucking in my little brother. Why does she do like that? And why do Mum and Dad hug in different ways?

Please tell me,

Peter

A letter from the nesting-box – reply from Björn

Hello there, Peter the Troll!

May I call you by that name? You do ask a lot of questions, just like those trolls in the Ronia story. Just like them, you rarely get a good reply! You have asked me many, many times why you come to see me, the sykoligist, as you call me. It cannot be easy for you. First of all, you have got all these "why-questions". Then, when you ask me, you get so few answers. As you see, I'm not good at answering all your why-questions. How should I explain this to you? Imagine that I'm sitting in a nesting-box in a tree in the woods. I'm listening to a troll named Peter, who keeps asking me a lot of questions: "Why are they doing like that, why aren't they doing like this?" I have discovered that it isn't very helpful for me to answer you, "They do like that because . . . or like this because. . ." The answers I would give you would just lead to a bunch of new questions and in the end you wouldn't be any wiser than you were in the beginning.

So I sit in my tree and listen to your questions. After I hear them, what I sometimes do is help you to ask them in a new way. Or, sometimes I remind you that you've asked the same question many times before. You've figured out the answer yourself but you've forgotten it. Then I wonder why you forget so easily – at least sometimes. At other times I would like to say to you, "You know the answer, Peter, but you get the sting when you think about it." I have learnt that the most difficult questions are the ones that create a sting inside us. Those are the questions that cause us pain. They hurt, somewhat like a bee-sting. That's why you keep on asking the same questions over and over again, because it hurts even more when you think about the answers. Everybody does this sometimes; we don't want to think about how the answers feel inside us. So we keep on asking, doing what we adults call "nagging". But children are not the only ones who nag in this way. Adults do it as well.

For example, you ask why your mother tucks your little brother into bed more than one time each night. You also ask why her voice sounds extra sweet when she speaks to him. I think you know the answer: Mummy loves your little brother in a way that makes her voice nice and sweet. Maybe you remember that she sounded that way with you before your little brother was born. I bet she used to say "Caro" to you too in those days. I know she was not referring to a car but to a darling. "Caro" means "Darling" in her language. Back then, you probably thought she loved you and *only* you. It was as if there were no other "Caro" in the whole world for her! Then your little brother was born and destroyed everything. But even before he was born, you probably understand now that while Mummy showed you lots of love, she showed other feelings, too. Sometimes I'm sure she was tired, annoyed or angry. And I don't think the *only* thing you feel about your brother today is anger. But that doesn't help you. You get the sting anyway, when you think about your mother's sweet voice when she is speaking to your little brother. You wonder, "Why is she doing like that?"

And why are your parents doing like they're doing? They send you to my office and I sit here in my nesting-box and I don't answer all the "why-questions" from Peter the troll. They're worried because you jump around in bed after they have said goodnight to you. They've told me that you pick fights with your brother and you hit him. Your dad said, "I don't want my son to become a troublemaker." He wanted me to make you become nicer now so that you wouldn't become a troublemaker later in life.

I couldn't promise your parents that I could make you become a nicer boy. And neither could I promise them that I could help you out right away. But when your mother told me that you often talk about having that sting inside when you start picking fights or nagging about something, I thought, "I think I can help that chap!" I know how it feels when you get that sting inside. It can happen to me as well; when I get angry or jealous or when someone has been nasty to me. I know that it's because of my feelings that I get that sting. So I thought it might be the same with you. I guessed that your feelings were causing that sting inside of you and that you needed to understand them better. That's why I thought I would be able to help you out. But I didn't think I could help you best by answering your question, "Why are they doing like that?" I thought it would be a better idea to find out – together with you – the answer to another question, "Why do I *feel* this way?"

Best wishes from the nesting-box,

Björn

Letter to the sykoligist from Peter

You nesting man!

Why do you do like that? Never answering my questions! You're just hiding in your nesting-box. I'm a little boy and you're somewhere up there, ten times higher and a hundred times stronger than I am. What are *your* secrets? As soon as I met you I started wondering about that. One time when I was sitting in your waiting room it sounded like you were on the phone. I thought I heard you laughing. You sounded nice and friendly, friendlier than you are with me. Then I thought about something else and I got that sting inside me. I thought that maybe you liked him more than me, even though I actually didn't know if the one on the phone was a boy or not. But this was the way I was thinking.

I could hardly wait until you opened the door after you'd finished your phone call. When you finally let me come in to your office, I said to you, or rather I yelled at you, "Who was that on the phone? Answer now! Who was it? Was it your child? Do you have any children? Tell me right this minute!" But you just said, "Well, you want to know whom I was speaking to on the phone and whether I have any children or not? Tell me more about it, Peter." Then I shouted, "You drive me crazy! Why can't you just answer?!" and threw a pencil at you. But all you could say was that you were still thinking about why I wanted to know if you have any children and a lot of other blablabla things. Like I said, you're just hiding inside the nesting-box. You think you're smart and cool sitting up there saying, "I'm thinking about what you're saying, Peter." But you aren't cool, you are soooooooo tiresome! Mum and Dad say that I drive them crazy but let me tell you something: you drive me crazy too!

But there's one good thing I have to say about you. You don't drive me crazy because I don't like you. Sorry, there were too many *nots*! I mean I . . . I think I like you. I have to tell you the truth, you're nice,

I've noticed that. It's because you don't get angry with me even though I get very rude and angry with you sometimes. But why do you have all those secrets? I asked Mum and she didn't know. She told me you're a sykoligist and that you know what you're doing. Now I'm asking the sykoligist: "Why are you doing like that?"

Grrrrrrr from Peter

Björn replies to Peter

Hi Peter!

You write about everything you don't know about me. And about how I just tend to answer blablabla whenever you ask me. Then you become cross with me. Well, why don't I want to tell you so much about myself? And why do you want to know all these things about me? Let's take the first question first. Perhaps you believe that I don't want to tell you whom I was speaking to, or if I have any children, just because these are such big secrets. But no, that's not the way it is. Is it because I want to be nasty and hurtful? This is how you imagine things sometimes. But that's not correct either. I do understand that it makes you sad to get so few answers from me. So why do I do like this?

I'd like to answer you this way: imagine a specially made nesting-box with a thousand passageways inside. Let's do a magic trick so that you become a tiny fellow, like one of those little trolls living in the underworld in Ronia's forest. Now, if you were to enter that nesting-box, what would you find out? You would be able to explore one or two of these passageways. But sooner or later you would lose your way and get dizzy. And as a matter of fact, you would not understand much of whatever you were able to explore. The reason is, and now I'm telling you something you maybe don't want to hear, that you're still a child.

Let's pretend that I was speaking to my wife on the phone that time when you were waiting outside my office. Why did I laugh or how did I laugh? Did I laugh the way Mum and Dad do on Saturday night when you are being sent to bed and they want to be alone with each other and hug in that special way? You know that adults sometimes want to do things and take care of things that are not meant for children, like what you and Charlie talked about, right? Or it may be money or weather or other issues. Okay, what if my wife and I were talking about such things? Remember how you told me that you, and by the way Charlie as well, don't always understand so much about what's going on with adults? Well, that's fine. After all, you're children. This is why I didn't answer you. If I did so, you would just ask more new questions and in the end you would get tangled up and lost in my answers and your new questions.

The second question was why you want to know everything about me. I think you want to know everything because the situation is not under your control. I've understood that whenever you can't control things, it hurts inside you and you get that sting. But, you know, no human being is ever completely able to control another human being, no matter how many questions he asks and how many answers he gets. That's why I've found another way of helping you. We can call it "training at the nesting-box". I want you to be able to wait when you don't understand. Wait until you've figured out for yourself what might have happened. Or, maybe instead you'll come up with a story about what might have happened.

Let's go back to that time when you rushed into my room and ordered me to tell you whom I was talking to on the phone. I told you that you probably became sad because you had to wait for me while you overheard me speaking on the phone. All of a sudden you said, "Sad things are hard." You looked serious and grieved. After a while you made up a telephone game. Each of us held a kind of telephone. You told me you were the boss at a space station and I was a spaceman. You taught me how to handle the steering wheel in order to fly the space shuttle safely through faraway stars. They were very dangerous, these stars, because they could explode any second. Then I thought, "Peter was able to make up a fun game instead of nagging and winding himself up. I guess that made him feel good." We might say you made up a space game while you were outside the nesting-box. We could also say that you were "wording" yourself up instead of winding yourself up like you do sometimes in bed or in other places. When you told me, "Sad things are hard," I thought to myself that words are a rather smart invention.

Let's also go back to what you wrote in your letter about your mother and her nice voice to your little brother. What would happen if you were to ask her, "Why do you get that soft voice when you're tucking little 'Caro' to bed?" She would maybe notice that you'd become sad and would answer, "Don't you know, Peter, that I love you as much as I love your little brother?" But would you believe her? Hardly! I guess you would say, "If you loved me as much as you love him, you would take a day off from work and take me to the zoo." But maybe Mum wouldn't agree because she can't leave work, and then you two would get into a quarrel. That's what almost happened to us that time when you wondered who was on the phone with me and then ordered me to answer all your questions. When you told me, "Sad things are hard" and when you made up the space game, I thought to myself, "Peter can make quite a fuss about things sometimes, but he is also a very likeable chap."

Best regards,

Björn

A letter from Peter on his way to the zoo

Hello Björn!

I don't have much time to write. It's Saturday and we're going to the zoo, Mum and I. She told me the other day that she had been thinking about our quarrel. You know, the one when she came back to my room because I made all those winding up noises and I asked her to read another chapter about Ronia. She told me that I had been very nasty then, but she understood that I wanted to be on my own with her and without my little brother. Can you imagine how happy she made me? I got this wave of niceness all over me. I told her, "Just because you're so nice and you're going to take me to the zoo, I promise I'll play with my little brother this afternoon so you can loosen up a little." I think I was very nice there, if I may say so myself. I felt a little like Dad when he tells her on Saturday nights that he'll put the children to bed and she can just sit there and loosen up.

But there's something I must tell you quickly before we take the bus to the zoo. Yesterday I wound myself up a bit in the kitchen while Mummy was feeding my little brother. You know, she was giving him her breast milk and I do *not* like it when she does that. Not at all. Mum told me to calm down and make a drawing instead. I scribbled a bit. She looked at the drawing and said, "Wow, Peter! What a good picture of a nesting-box! Such cute little nestlings you have drawn inside that box!" I made the entire drawing without thinking a second. First I got happy because Mum liked my drawing. Then I got annoyed because she said the nestlings were cute. So I added an eagle hovering above the nesting-box. I made its beak very sharp and awesome. Mum asked what it was. "It's an eagle. It . . . is flying around a little, hovering just to check things out," I said. "Aha," Mum replied, but I don't think she really got it.

Actually I had thought of having the eagle swoop towards the nesting-box and grab one of the nestlings and eat it. But then I thought another animal might come along and defend the nestlings. Or it might call for the bird mum or dad so that they could come and chase the eagle away. Then the nestlings would make it, after all, and go on living. Can a couple of bird parents chase away an eagle? In a way I don't think so, but in a way I think if they worked together, the eagle might not stand a chance. Anyhow, I do know who *you* think would be the winner. But I won't tell you! I'll bring that drawing next time we meet at your office. Then, if you ask me who would win, the bird parents or the eagle, I'll do exactly the same as you always do with me. I'll put a mysterious look on my face and ask you, "Weeeell, Björn, what do *you* think yourself?"

See you soon,

Peter

Chapter 4

Raging with love

Hello Majlis!

My name is Alma. I'm six years old. Well, almost. I answer six whenever anybody asks me. I think that sounds better. I don't want to be a little child any longer and I am not one either, by the way. I am about to be promoted at school. I'm writing to you because I'm so angry. Everybody makes decisions for me and chooses stuff for me above my head. I am not allowed to make any choice by myself, and this is why I'm so angry! I'm angry almost all the time. But I'll start from the beginning.

I don't know much about the very beginning of my life. I was so small then. But when I was two years old, my mother and my father split up – I can remember that. At least, I remember I went to another house and Mum and I were supposed to sleep there. But I didn't want to. I didn't like that new place, not one bit. It was so cold and dark. You see, even in those days they didn't let me decide anything at all! They just went in different directions and I couldn't do anything but tag along. Nowadays, I live mostly with my mother, but sometimes I live with my father during weekends. Then his lady friend is there as well. He calls her "his fiancée". I don't like that word. It reminds me of an old lady who lives next door, called Fiona. She has a grumpy voice and ugly teeth and I don't like her. So now, you understand why I don't like Dad's fiancée either. I don't want her to live there, I mean at my daddy's place.

Now they think I'm causing them trouble and they say I need to see a psychologist. I don't want to. I want to decide for myself. What's a psychologist by the way? Could you please tell me because they say you are such a person. Mummy helped me to write the word properly. She pronounces it *sykologist* but she tells me it should be written with a P in the beginning. Is that right?

Best wishes from Alma.

P.S. Wait, I just remembered something important! Sometimes I suddenly need to pee, more than other kids, it seems like. Like at the playground. I need to rush to the loo and then the other kids tease me. They call me "Alma PG". As if I didn't understand that they mean that I'm a Pee Girl! If I rush to the loo at your place, it'll be because I need to pee. Do you have a loo or will I have to go back home and pee? Can I come back to your place when I'm finished?

Reply from Majlis

Hello Alma!

It does sound troublesome not to be able to decide for yourself. The grown-ups decide all the time and you're little. Perhaps you're getting angry right now because I call you "little". After all, you are almost six years old. Well, it's true that when you are six you aren't little, but still, you're not as big as the grown-ups!

It was a good idea of yours to ask me what psychologist means. A psychologist is someone who talks with somebody who is having trouble. Yes, your mum's right – it is spelled with a P. Some people have a hard time pronouncing it. Once I even heard someone saying it so quickly that it sounded like "cyclist", as if she were riding a bicycle! They say you're troublesome. I don't know you so well yet, so I don't know if you're causing trouble. But I do know that you're *having* trouble. Being angry almost all the time is troublesome to anyone. And you tell me that sometimes you don't know what is making you angry. That is one of those things you and I could try to find out. But for now, let's wait until we meet in a few days. I just heard from your mother that you are coming to my office on Thursday and that you, Alma, made the decision.

So keep well until Thursday. Then we'll learn more if I can help you and we'll talk about old ladies and fiancées and other things, too. Well, if you want to, of course. Another thing about a psychologist, she's someone who just lets people talk about what they want. But obviously, you cannot speak right out into empty air, so I will also have some things to say to you. Let's see what we want to say, each one of us, on Thursday.

See you soon,

Majlis
P.S. I do have a loo. Of course, it's okay for you to use it when you need to.

Response to a lady with pink towels

Hello Majlis!

Now I have been to your place. As a matter of fact, it has been quite a few times now. What an odd name you've got, Majlis. I don't know anyone with that name. I don't know anyone like you, either. When I first saw your room I thought it had so many weird things in it. But it was cool that you allowed me to play with them. Your loo is also supercool. I liked your pink towels. Did you know that? Maybe it was when I saw those towels that I decided to come back to you. At first, it was difficult for me to pronounce your name. Then I thought, "She's my Liss" and suddenly I knew how to pronounce it. Easy peasy! Now I've got my own toy box in your room. I keep everything that we use in that box. I'd like to talk about that doll I call "Strong Adolf" and his car, the little doll Mimi and the train, and then the airplane that I made myself. What happened actually the last time we played with them?

You usually say that we can talk about it next time. But this time is different. I'm going away to my grandma's. I guess I won't see you for a long time and I'm wondering about so many things. Please, please tell me what really happened! When I left you the other day, I remembered quite a lot about it, but then on the underground Dad and Fiona – sorry, his fiancée – just sat there blabbing away and suddenly I couldn't remember anything at all about what you and I had been doing! Well, almost nothing at all. Oh sekoor, sillvoo play. (A French boy just started at my preschool. His name is Jean. That's how I learnt to speak French.)

So long from Alma

Response from Majlis

Hello Alma!

You're right – we have been seeing each other for some time now. So many things happened when we played together last time. I'll tell you what I remember and you can see what you think of my story. Then we will talk about it when we meet next time.

This is the way I recall the game we played together. At first you flew round with that plane of yours for a while. Then the game with "Strong Adolf" and "Little Mimi" started. These two characters have been part of our games for quite some time. This time you told me that Little Mimi was whispering something to Strong Adolf: "Why don't we get married?" But he was busy driving his car and just hissed at her, "Shut up, you little girl, I'm going to look at the airplane." Then you flew about alone with the airplane as if you were the strongest of them all. You looked very cocky and cool. But then you changed the story and gave Strong Adolf and Mimi the opposite feelings. Adolf wanted to marry Mimi but she didn't want it any more. You told me, "He just said 'My darling, my beloved woman.'" It sounded funny when you imitated Adolf whispering to Mimi. But she got very angry and didn't want to marry him at all. She jumped on the train and rode away and left him. Adolf followed the train with his car. It was a terrific chase. They drove round and round. It looked as if they were on a TV show. You pretended now and then to be Mimi, like when you whispered, "Should we get married?" Sometimes you pretended to be a strong adult and looked very bold. Those things kept changing back and forth. For me, it was not easy to follow you. To tell you the truth, it was quite tricky.

Then you changed the story again. You mentioned a big doll and told me, "This is her mummy." I guess you meant Mimi's mother. I found it difficult to keep track of everything, believe it or not! Anyway, this mother was about to have a baby. Strong Adolf caught sight of Mimi again and was still really in love. But then you said, "Her mother spoke to Mimi about him and she got frightened." And then Little Mimi left Strong Adolf, who tried to get her back. And then you sighed, "But he was just in love, he couldn't help it." I was thinking of those TV series, not the kind where people chase and shoot each other all the time, but love stories, where a girl is desperate to get a certain boy but is afraid she will never succeed. Maybe you haven't seen stories like this on TV or in movies. But if you think about the fairy tale of Cinderella, I guess you understand what I mean. Remember when she is standing by the window, longing to go to the ball at the royal palace? Remember the prince everybody is talking about? Cinderella thinks it would be wonderful to have him as a husband, but she is afraid she has no chance!

These thoughts invaded my head as soon as I heard your sighs. The story you told me was quite a sad one. Little Mimi ran away. She was angry and she was afraid. Everything happened at the same time. There were really a lot of feelings going around! This is how things might be when you've got a lot of feelings inside, all at the same time. Sometimes you feel as if there is not enough space for them inside. But it seems that things have become easier since you have started coming to me. I think that's because you haven't had to keep all these feelings inside yourself so long anymore, only up to our next meeting. To be honest with you, I know it may be rough sometimes for you to meet me, to pour out all these feelings, so to speak. And then, you must leave and go back home again. When you receive this letter, you will be at your grandmother's place, so you'll have to wait longer than usual before we meet again. It'll be next week.

Regards from Majlis

Reply to somebody who is a bit weird

Majlis!
Now things are weird. You know how I say that you can be weird sometimes. You talk about things people don't care to talk about and then you ask me what I think. But now things are weird in other ways.

Last weekend I was with Daddy and Yvonne. She is his fiancée, the one I told you about before. His "Fiona" as I call her. I've been at their place many times before, but this time things were different. I enjoyed being with them. Usually I wanted to be by myself there, or with either with Dad or with Fiona – but never with the two of them at the same time. When she and I are together she's not too bad! Yes, I really mean it. This time when we were there the three of us, it was cosy. We watched TV and I was allowed to stay up longer than usual. When the film was over, Dad told me it was time to go to bed. I didn't put up a fight. I thought he was right – that's quite odd, isn't it? But it was also cosy to hide myself under my covered duvet, the duvet I chose myself at IKEA. It's pink. When I was about to choose it, Daddy told me any colour would do. He told me, "We'll tuck it into a cover, so you won't see it anyway. Take the grey one, it's cheaper." That's the way he put it. He thinks he's so smart but sometimes he just doesn't get it. He doesn't understand that I could lie in my bed and feel quite cosy, thinking, "Here, under Daddy and Yvonne's duvet cover thingy is my own duvet. It's pink because I chose it myself."

I got really angry with Daddy at IKEA. I think it was last winter. In those days I was always cross – well, most of the time. I felt like I had a superangry ball inside me. There were spikes on it. Then I started seeing you and after a while, the ball got smaller, kind of. I don't know how to put it. I guess I still get angry when Sarah teases me at school, but I don't get angry the way I used to. Back then I got so angry I didn't know what to do. It was very hard on me. Like the time I stamped on the pink duvet at IKEA when Dad said I should buy the cheap one. It was grey and white checked. Phew! How ugly it was! When I was stamping Daddy said, "We'll have to buy that pink duvet after all, now that you've dirtied it." He was annoyed and didn't talk to me at all the rest of the day. As for me, I was as happy as I could be with my pink duvet. Well, okay, I was ashamed, too. You and I have talked about how I got my way that time, you know.

Another thing I was thinking about, concerning Daddy and Yvonne. I notice from time to time that they want to be alone. Then I get sad because I'm not allowed to be with them. So I get angry. I like them, and I feel sad and angry all at the same time. Now I'm wondering, why is that superangry ball getting smaller nowadays? Is it because I have been visiting you and we've been playing together? I think this would be your answer. It sounds funny. Daddy says it's because I'm a big girl now. Who's right? You or Dad?

Bye-bye from Alma
P.S. See you next week, but please answer earlier!

A typical psychologist response

Hello Alma!

I'll give a typical psychologist answer. I think both of us, your dad and I, are right. You're on your way to becoming bigger now, and you're able to do a lot of things you didn't do before. But I believe it's also because of all the things we've been talking about and playing at. We've been arguing and laughing at all these things for a while now, you and I. And let us not forget the main character – *you*! You are really working hard, not only when we see each other but also when you're on your own. We've been seeing each other all winter, and soon you'll be promoted at school. You're wondering why you're feeling so different now compared to when you started to see me. And then you wonder if it has helped you to see me. Well, it seems so.

Why is it that you feel better, not only because you are a bigger girl now, but also because of our playing and talking? Let's take Strong Adolf and Little Mimi as an example. In my last letter I wrote that it seemed that Adolf was in love with Mimi but she left him. At first, she wanted to marry him. Then she got afraid and angry. We said that a person can have many feelings all at the same time. This is true not only for your games but for you as well. You have made it clear to me that you've got many feelings inside, all at the same time. We might take your feelings about Dad or Yvonne as an example. You wrote to me that you feel cosy, sad and angry when you are with them. You see, there is that inside mix again!

I think it takes time to really understand that we can have so many different feelings when we are with other people, like you have when you're with Dad and Yvonne. This means that you've got to think about it very often. You know how I always say, "We have to work on this." I know that you think it sounds funny when I say that we are working together, but actually we are. You tell me that we're playing games, and that's true as well. Oops, there you got another psychologist answer: "You're right and I'm right."

You've been playing at Strong Adolf and Little Mimi. You keep adding something new to the game, and every time we understand a little bit more about why you have been having trouble. I'm especially thinking about last week. Do you remember? You brought out Strong Adolf and his little car and Little Mimi and the train once again. This time Adolf started to chase Mimi. You told me he was crying out for love: "My Loooooove." And you told me, "Here comes Adolf, raging with love." Strong Adolf was running after Little Mimi, crying, "Open, open up!" And the little doll answered, "Never, I'll never open up for *you*." You put Little Mimi on the train. Strong Adolf jumped into his car and followed Little Mimi. First the train and then the car. And then you told me he got tired of it all. There were only "hearts in the air, not those bold snakes and all those things", as you put it. Adolf was fed up with things that were only for girls, you said. He didn't get into the train.

Wow! I was dying to know what was coming next! What kinds of hearts were flying about in the air? And those bold snakes, I'd never heard about them before! When you said "bold", I thought of how "un-bold" you were when we met for the first time. You were afraid, thinking I didn't have any loo and that you'd need to go back to your mum's place to pee. You were also scared that I'd tease you about it, just like your friends did when they called you Alma PG.

Anyway, Adolf and Mimi were about to marry now, even though she had said, "I'll never do it!" They even wanted to have a church wedding. To get to the church, Mimi was allowed to sit up on the roof of the car while Adolf was manoeuvring and driving. On the way there, a lot of things happened and the car went off the road. Mimi fell off and Adolf fell out, and in the end, the wedding never took place.

All these events were made up by you in the story game. As for myself, I was sitting next to you, wondering what you were trying to tell me through all your eventful stories. The Adolf and Mimi story was very similar to what I wrote in my previous letter. You are indeed thinking deeply about what it means to like or love someone, and to be angry with that person at the same time. Through your expression, "Adolf was raging with love" and the things we talked about afterwards, I understood one thing very clearly: if Strong Adolf was raging with love, he might just as well be you! Imagine! Does it mean that you're enraged and in love, all at the same time? It looks like it. I think you can love your dad simply because he's your dad and, at the same time, be disappointed or angry because he lives with Yvonne.

There's another thing I'm wondering about. You told me in your letter that you didn't put up a fight when Dad and Yvonne told you to go to bed. You felt the time was right for them to be alone. Was it because they're adults and you're a child? Maybe you thought it was okay to be little for a while. Right now you're little, but you're growing up all the time. Let's talk about that next time we meet.

Until then, keep well!

Majlis

All this talking! Reply from Alma

Majlis!

All this talk about feelings! And that thing about being little! Well, maybe that's the way it is, but I want to grow up and become an adult – now.

Do you know, I've found out about a new feeling I didn't have before! I call it the tingle feeling. It was like this. I was with Dad and Yvonne last weekend. I was playing with Elizabeth, who lives next door. She told me a new family had moved into their building. We were stealing around, trying to get a glimpse of the newcomers. Suddenly, we saw a boy coming out of the building. He came right up to us! He told us his name was Dawit, and then we played, all three of us, all afternoon. This is when I got the tingle feeling. It kind of tingled inside me. He was so cute. He talked a bit funny but he has not been in our country very long. He comes from Eri . . . , bah! I don't remember the name of his country. Anyway it was really nice to play with him.

So long! See you on Monday.

Alma

Chapter 5

Here comes Pippi Lundström

Dear Father!

Do sit down in your cabin and get ready for some fun because here comes a letter from your daughter! I'm writing so quickly that my pencil is glowing red. I've got so many things to tell you. There are two children, Tommy and Annika, who just moved into the house next door. Can you imagine how happy I am? When no one lived there it always made our house seem gloomy and dark, too. But now things are different. Every afternoon they come here and play. It's really easy to play with them. First of all, because we are about the same age, and second, they don't make a fuss when I decide which games to play. As you know, I like to decide. So, we get along well.

What kind of games did we play today? Well, first we had to clean up my room! Mum asked me to do it (grrrr). Well, "ask" is not the right word. As a matter of fact, she rushed into my room without even knocking. She used that awful tone of voice. "It looks terrrrrrribble. Tidy up your room right now, it's driving me maaaaad!" I think she likes to make certain words superlong just to be sure to screw them into my head. I guess she thinks that'll make me do as I have been told. Anyway, I looked around my room. She was right. There were a lot of things I had forgotten to put away. But then I got a great idea – we could make it into a game. I told Tommy and Annika that we were going to make ourselves into thing-pick-uppers!

You just can't imagine what sort of things we found! For instance, we found my old T-shirt from last summer. I thought I had lost it somewhere. It's yellow with stripes and it looks a bit exotic, maybe like a tiger. Annika wondered where it came from. I told her that you are a sea captain and that you bought it for me while you were on a trip to the Cape of Good Hope in Africa. They had never even heard of the place! But that didn't stop them from claiming that I was lying to them. I got mad and told them you are often at sea for many months. I also told them that you send me gifts all the time and that you really long to get back to your daughter. But, alas, your job prevents you from being with me as much as you would like to. After all, that's what you tell me when I ask you why you work so much.

Annika still didn't want to believe me when I told her the shirt was made in Africa. She said she could swear I bought it at H&M and started looking for some label inside the neckband. I told her to stop it and then we had a quarrel. Tommy told her that I was only lying on pretence. I think that was a clever way of putting things, don't you? Then I told Annika that a person like me, whose mother is an angel up in heaven and whose father is a sea captain, can't be expected to tell the exact boring truth all the time. But she went right on giving me a hard time and said, "Well, your mother just came in here to your room and asked you to clean it up, didn't she?" I explained to her that the person was not my mother but a servant you had sent from Africa because you wanted to give me more time to do my homework. At this point, Annika finally shut up and looked like she was thinking over what I said. Tommy smiled and said, "Imagine having my own servant! Then I would never have to wash the dishes or do all the other stupid things that Mum keeps asking me to do."

It took us a long time to tidy up the room because of all that talking about your being a sea captain or not. Then suddenly Annika's and Tommy's mother showed up at our place. She told them that dinner was ready and it was time to go back home. While she was talking to Mum, she got that kind of worried look on her face that certain people get when they are talking to Mum. Maybe they think something's wrong with her, that she's not well. Maybe they think something's wrong with me, too. But there's nothing wrong with me. I feel great! I just started my third year at school. I've got two new friends next door and a daddy who is a sea captain and who loves me more than anything on earth. Could things be better?

Well, what do you have to say about all this? I'd like to know! Your daughter,

Pippilotta Comestibles Windowshade Curlymint Ephraimsdaughter Longstocking

The father replies

Dear Hanna!

Well, well, you do have a wild imagination, don't you? What a funny name you've got! If you are called Ephraimsdaughter, I guess I'm Ephraim. I wonder what they would say at work if I started to sign the invoices with my new name: "Ephraim Lundström". This week I'm in Gothenburg a couple of days. I forgot my cell phone charger so I have not been able to call you. But all is well with me. Thanks for all the news about how things are with you. It sounds delightful that Annika and Tommy moved in next door. Don't be hurt if Annika doesn't believe you. After all, you've always had a lively imagination. By the way, are their names really Annika and Tommy? Or is that something you took from your books about Pippi Longstocking?

It worries me when you say the neighbour gave Mum that look, like maybe she's not feeling well. I guess that's why she sounded irritated when she asked you to clean up your room. I think you should do what Mummy tells you to do. I know fully well that you didn't want us to get divorced. I also know that you say you like it better at my place because I'm nicer to be with than your mother. Or perhaps, it's simply because I'm not as demanding as she is when it comes to housework. But, anyhow, Mum is the one to decide about cleaning up at *her* place and I'm the one to do so at *my* place. It was not easy for me to leave your mother. I shouldn't talk with you about these things by the way, because then I'd have to mention Beatrice and I know you don't want me to do that. To make it brief, all I meant to say is that the nicer you are with your mother, the happier she gets and the happier I get. Do I sound too much like a bossy daddy now?

Aha, I'm a sea captain and I've even been to the Cape of Good Hope! Well, if you say so, I won't object. In that case we need a cook's helper in the galley kitchen on my ship. After all, we have a crew who need to eat and drink. Could you consider taking on that position? With a substantial wage, I promise. The other day, my boss told me how much he gives his daughter for her weekly allowance. She gets 150 kronor per week. I couldn't afford that, but what about increasing yours from 75 to 100? Could you consider my offer to be our cook's helper on the seven seas? Think about it and let's talk when I go back home.

Big hugs from Daddy – sorry, from Captain Ephraim Lundström.

Reply from Pippi

Dear Father!

Thank you for your bulletin from the seven seas. And thanks for raising my weekly allowance. Well done, Captain! However, about your offer for me to work as a cook's helper on your ship, I am afraid I can't accept it. I would rather be the first mate standing next to the captain on the deck whenever a storm is raging and a gigantic bolt of lightning is threatening to split the ship in two and difficult decisions have to be made instantly. Gothenburg – in what part of Africa do you find that harbour? How long will it take for you to reach your next port of destination and when will you be sailing for home again? I guess it depends on the winds – whether they will be fair or whether you'll have to beat the trade wind. As you see, I love geography. I love learning the names of faraway places and exciting people.

But otherwise school is not much fun. The most difficult of all is maths, plus the way that two girls in my class keep bullying me because my parents are divorced. I always say to myself, "Just you wait! One of these days you'll be in the same situation, and then let's see who'll get the last laugh." Up to now, their parents are still living together, and have not drifted apart like mine have. That's why they tease me.

I have loads of trouble with maths. I understand things when I'm able to put my fingers on them. For instance, when the teacher asks me what $7 + 3$ makes, it's easy for me to answer. I just fetch a box of matches and then I count them and find the right answer. Ten, right, Captain? However, why $7 \times 8 = 53$, that's not easy for me to see. Of course, you could make seven stacks with eight matches in each. But then you're supposed to count them all, and all of a sudden one or two matches fall on the floor and you've got to start counting them all over again.

The other day I lost my temper during my maths lesson. I told my teacher that I'd had enough of her fartification tables. I thought she'd get very cross with me because I was yelling. Instead she smiled and told me that the correct word was multification, or, did she say mulplication? I don't remember. She also said she was going to get a remedial teacher for me. I don't really know what she meant, but I do know what's going to happen: more homework! Of course, the girls I told you about grabbed the chance to bully me once more because I had said fartification. They made funny fart-like noises with their lips pressed together and had loads of fun. I just glared at them.

Well, never mind the girls. I was in a hurry to go home because Mum had promised to make cinnamon buns. She always wants me to go home from school straightaway even though she never looks very happy when I get there. She looks grey and then she smiles, but she doesn't smile with her eyes! Do you know why her eyes can look so strange, so tired? Even though you left Mum and me and now you stick together with that Beatrice of yours, could you help me to understand this, Dad? By the way, I think Beatrice should change her glasses. She looks so, well, so over the top when she wears them. But don't tell her I said so.

Warms regards from your daughter,

Pippilotta Comestibles Windowshade Curlymint Ephraimsdaughter Longstocking.

P.S. Of course, the new neighbour kids are Tommy and Annika. What did you imagine? That Tommy was Annika and Annika Tommy? Seriously, Captain, what's going on up there in your wheelhouse?

Response from Gothenburg and not from Africa

Dear Pippi C.W.C.E. Longstocking,

I'm sorry that I haven't written out your name in full but I'm in a hurry. We sailors, sorry, salesmen have a meeting just outside Gothenburg and I must be there on time. Okay, I'm still a sea captain and Tommy is Tommy and Annika is Annika. Agreed, let's have it that way, but I do have to tell you that Gothenburg is five hundred kilometres west of Stockholm. You say you love geography, but apparently this only applies to Africa and other faraway places. It's quite clear that you dislike multiplication. Why 7 x 8 = 56 and not 53 is difficult to explain, I will admit. I guess that once upon a time, some people agreed on that point and then we all just have to accept it and learn it by heart. Okay, I know you never like to do things just because you're told to do so. You're being independent, and that's a good thing most of the time but not when it comes to learning the multiplication tables.

When Mum tells you to go home from school straightaway, well, I guess that's the kind of thing you just have to do, like the multiplication tables. You asked me why your mother doesn't look happy. Let me explain it a little: when Mum and I met, she was a happy and beautiful young lady. I fell in love with her at first sight. She was very hard-working and wanted everything to be correct and complete. I was quite proud of all that she accomplished, I want you to know. A few years before your birth, she had a "burnout". It doesn't mean that she burnt herself in the kitchen or anything like that. No, she had been working too hard. She had a demanding boss and couldn't say no to him. That made her sad and tired, and finally she had to take a sick leave. But after a while she got well again.

Everything was sunny again and we decided to have a baby. When you were in your mother's belly, she was happy and looked forward to giving birth. I'm certain she was jubilant when she first saw you looking up at her with your bright blue eyes. But it turned out that as a little baby you spent much more time crying than we had expected. Mummy was nervous. Maybe you cried because you didn't like the way it felt when she was so nervous. I don't know which came first, your crying or her "postnatal depression", as the health visitor at our child health centre used to call it when Mum was really down. Afterwards, Mum explained to me that nobody could understand what was going on. Depression means roughly that you're sad and don't find any fun in life at all. Her mother, your grandmother, kept saying you were a screamer of a baby and nobody but your mum could stand to be near you with your incessant crying. She also used to say that your mother was an angel for being able to stand you. When Grandmother spoke that way Mum got sad and I got angry. Your mummy had guilt feelings – well, me too, actually. She felt guilty because she was not happy, and I felt guilty because I was working too much.

One year later you started day care. Mum went back to work and life resumed its daily course. But between Mum and me, it seemed like we couldn't get back to the good times we used to have. We did try to make things better, believe me. First, we moved to that semi-detached house. A little later we took a holiday trip to Madeira. Then we got our kitten, Mickey. You still love Mickey very much. But as for the love between Mum and me, it seemed to have left the house. Towards the end, I couldn't take it any longer and decided to leave her. Now I have my new life with Beatrice and I feel like things have worked out well for me. But I guess your mum has never quite got over it, and this is what you see in her eyes. I can't give you any advice except to try to understand her – and wait until I get back home. Next week as usual, you'll stay with me and we'll have some fun. I just heard from another salesman at my office that a skating rink has been built outside the city and there'll be some shows there. Should we go for it? It could be cool! Damn it! Now I'm late! I wrote too long a letter. I'm always late for those salesmen's meetings. Me, always nagging at you to go to school on time, maybe I should follow my own advice!

Your father, Captain Lundström from Gothenburg and its surroundings

One more answer from Pippi

Dear Father!

You're a funny guy! Gothenburg is not located by any African ocean. I checked it in my geography book! So what are you doing in our vast country, when you ought to be facing the wide horizons or planning your next voyage? You can keep on talking about salesmen's meetings as much as you like, but I'll believe whatever I want to believe. I told Annika and Tommy that you and I disagree about what your job really is. Tommy said that his father also goes to salesmen's meetings. "There, do you see now? He doesn't believe you and I don't either!" Annika snapped, looking very cheeky. But I told her straightaway, "If you don't believe that my father is a sea captain, I'll test you on the entire multiplication table and then you won't be able to watch the children's program on TV." Did you notice that I used the proper word this time? "Multiplication!" That settled the matter, Annika kept quiet and we played storms at sea. I think this game was perfect for a seafarer's daughter, don't you? Of course, my room ended up looking like it had been hit by the storm and Mum came rushing in saying . . . Well, you can imagine yourself what she said! But then we made up a story that we had to go to Tommika's (I'm quite smart at inventing new abbreviations, if I may say so myself!) house and fetch something and that we would clean up my room later.

So we sat there in Tommika's kitchen and their mother asked us if we wanted some sweets. She has got such smooth hands! And her eyes are bright and smiling all the time. When she asked how things were at school today, I answered that in Argentina kids don't have to go to school. It's against the law to give kids homework. Instead there is a pipeline feeding them with candy from a factory nearby. She smiled and said she had read about that too in a book. Then she looked at the kitchen table, where she had the bowl of sweets she was talking about. She asked about my mother. I took two candies and, as always, I said, "Thank you, she's fine, and how are you?" Then I put one sweet in my mouth. The other one I kept inside my hand until it was time to go back home.

It was cool to read what you wrote about how things were when I was a small child, even though I don't understand everything. I don't recall so much, but I do remember a lot of talk about angels when Granny used to visit us. I remember she used to call me angel and glare at me in an angry way at the same time. I didn't like that.

Last night I dreamt I was a sea captain on an icebreaker. We crossed the sea at such a high speed that the seagulls couldn't keep pace with us. You were the first mate and obeyed my orders. Do I even need to tell you that I was the captain? All of a sudden I saw an iceberg. There was not enough time to steer away from it. While all this was going on, an angel was slowly flying over the ship. It was like the angel had been trapped inside this iceberg and now she was free. I woke up and heard myself screaming, "Mummy". I guess it was a nightmare. I got out of bed, drank some water, went to the loo and then got back in bed. It was quite cool to be the sea captain instead of you! Then I started to think about the angel. It was strange crashing into the iceberg and at the same time seeing the angel being released from it. I thought about it for a while and then I fell asleep again. Now I'm longing for Sunday, when you come back from the Congo River!

Your daughter, Captain (ha-ha) Pippilotta Comestibles Windowshade Curlymint Ephraimsdaughter Longstocking.

Another reply from the father

Dear Hanna,

What a dream! It seems you found your iceberg adventure fun and frightening at the same time. Just wait until we meet next week. Then we'll see who is the captain and who is the first mate! First mate – can we call a girl a first mate? Anyway, I hereby appoint you first mate of my simple abode. I wonder what Beatrice is going to say. And what kind of job she is going to have on our ship. I guess if I give her that cook's helper job which you declined, she will be very cross with me. I must find a solution . . .

Now that you've written about your dream, I'd like to tell you about mine last night! I was standing on a huge clock located on the top of a big tower. Even though I was standing on it, I could touch it with my hands. I held both hands of the clock tightly, which made the clock go backwards. A policeman yelled at me to get down straightaway. He checked my driving licence. When he looked at it, he burst out laughing and said, "Okay, Captain!" Then I woke up and thought, "What if I could make time go backwards and do everything right, all those things that I did once, and which turned out to be bad? There would be no overtime work for me and no burnt food for you. And, you know, maybe there wouldn't be any divorces either."

Well, like you say, dreams can give us lots to think about. See you on Sunday at any rate. I'll pick you up at five o'clock as usual. Don't forget to bring another sweater. Winter is coming and it'll be quite cold in that newly built ice rink.

Your father, captain of the Seven Seas and Eight Offices.

Chapter 6

You'll be deader than dead

Hello Majlis!

Do you remember me? My name is Emma and I am twelve years old. Actually, I'll be thirteen next week. But when I used to come to see you I was much younger, eight or nine years old, I believe. I don't remember much about what we talked about then, but I do remember that I made a lot of drawings. I still like to make drawings. We have moved to another flat, but, luckily, I am still in my old class because we didn't move that far. I have many friends in my class and we have a great time.

But something happened recently and it's troubling me. So I thought it might be a good idea to write to you. In a way, I still think of you as my psychologist. This is the way it goes: I've become afraid of ghosts. Well, not real ghosts exactly, but I am terrified of dead people and, most of all, of skulls.

I don't know when it all started. I remember that on one of my visits to you, I made a drawing and I think it was a skull. Back then I was afraid such things would sneak into my room. Nowadays I'm not afraid in the same way. But I'm still very afraid, though I'm not able to "pin it down", if you know what I mean. Oscar, my big brother, if you remember, teases me about it. The other day, he and his pals were watching a horror movie on a DVD and when it got very scary they called me, "Come on, Emma, come see something really funny!" I peeped at the TV screen and I got dead scared. I saw an old lady in a wheelchair, and when she turned around, she was just a skeleton with a skull on top of it. I ran out of the room as fast as I could – and the boys all laughed and called me a psycho. When you and I met some years ago, I recall that we were talking about thoughts – all the time! Now I wonder myself why I get these thoughts. Why can't I stop thinking about all these skulls?

I also remember thinking my classmates were really bratty. Today, many of them have become my friends. For instance, I like Karen a lot. She's my best friend now. Imagine, Karen, the girl I hated most of all in the whole world! Do you remember when I didn't speak to my classmates? I used to sit alone in the schoolyard, dead silent. I was thinking about a lot of things that were so difficult to talk about – till I met you eventually. I told you about the terrible thoughts that I had in the schoolyard. Actually I wanted to blast off the heads of all my schoolmates and I didn't dare to tell anybody! I didn't even dare to tell myself, so to say. I mean, every time I was sitting there silent, all those thoughts blasted my head off, almost. Then I just had to run out of the schoolyard.

I guess I was an odd person the way I would sit quite motionless in the schoolyard and suddenly dash off. I did that for a long time, maybe a year. On the little road opposite the schoolyard there were some trees. I used to climb up one of those trees and wait for them to disappear: I mean those thoughts about shooting my classmates. My teacher would notice what I was doing. She got concerned and asked me if I had been harassed. I guess I hadn't been, actually. The girls weren't nasty to me. It was rather I who was being cruel to them – but only in my imagination! Then there was a meeting with the school psychologist and a lot of hullaballoo. But I never told anyone what I was actually thinking: that I wanted to shoot them all and that I hated myself for thinking that way. Like I said, in those days I didn't even dare to think or to admit it to myself. I guess I had been sitting at the school psychologist's office for quite a while when she finally said, "I think I'm going to call someone called Majlis. You could talk to her if you feel like it." I wasn't sure I felt like talking to a lady I had never met. But after all I could give it a try, I told myself.

I can joke about it a little today, but in those days I just wanted to get away from it all. I discovered that the lady called Majlis – you, I mean – was easier to talk to than I had thought. So, things got a bit easier at school. Sometimes, things even got really fun and interesting. But right now, when I was sure life had got better again, what's happened to me? I've become afraid of skulls again! Please answer me quickly and tell me why I'm so afraid! This is really, really bothering me.

So long,

Emma
P.S. I hope you're feeling fine.
P.P.S. By the way, have you still got that drawing of the skull? Could I see it?

Reply from Majlis

Hello Emma!
Of course, I remember you. It's good to hear that you've made friends with your classmates. But I understand that those thoughts about skulls

and death are really troubling you. I'll tell you how I recall things that we spoke about, what you told me and how you felt.

You could be quite angry sometimes and say, "You'll be deader than dead!" You got really angry with a lot of people. You wanted to shoot them down one after the other so that they would become "dead for sure", as you put it. Do you remember when you were so angry with Karen because she had been teasing you? You had bought a new pair of jeans and you were very proud of them, but she said they were ugly. After you heard that, you kept on thinking, "Karen, you'll be deader than dead." Then you became afraid of her. It was almost as if Karen was already dead and that she had lost her life because of you. But Karen-deader-than-dead also became a kind of character inside your head. It was as if some kind of a manga character of Karen was occupying your schoolyard and your head. I suggested that perhaps one could compare this inside-Karen to people appearing on the theatre stage or the TV screen.

You wrote in your letter that in those days, you hated yourself so much because you were thinking about these terrible things. But you hardly knew about it yourself. You'd rather talk about another character called "Emma-will-die". It was as if you were going to be punished because of all your terrible thoughts about Karen and the other girls. And then you told me, "That girl, Emma-will-die, she wants me to die." This character did not want you to exist since you had been such a bad person with your awful thoughts inside. Of course, I used to wonder why you had those thoughts and why you thought you would have to be killed because of them.

We talked about all these things, and we noticed that you were very afraid when you got angry. In those days, you believed that if you were thinking about something it was the same thing as if you were doing it for real. For example, if you were thinking that Karen was bratty and unkind and that she ought to be "deader than dead", then in your mind it was as if Karen were already dead! Of course, that would be scary indeed. Should that happen, the only suitable punishment for you would be death, according to the way your thoughts went. This might seem logical, but of course it's not correct. To think and to act are two different things. Plus, you were being very hard on yourself by seeing a death sentence as the right punishment for having scary thoughts.

I believe you know all this today. But now you're afraid of skulls. I already have a guess: you're angry with somebody or something. So far, we don't know much more than that.

In your letter you asked about the drawing you made when you were nine. I still have it, and here is a copy that I'm sending with this letter for you to look at.

46 You'll be deader than dead

I wonder what you think about it today. After all, it has been four years now since we last saw each other.

Best regards from Majlis

What a picture!

Hello Majlis!

Mama mia, what a picture! I remember exactly now! I was so angry then. Nobody knew about it. The funny thing is that I didn't know it myself. Now that I look at the picture I think it's strange I drew some hair. After all, a skull doesn't have any hair; it's as bald-headed as an ice-skating rink! If you look at it, it doesn't really look that terrible. But in those days, I was so afraid of it. I remember when I was falling asleep, the skulls used to enter my head. I knew they were not there for real. The window was closed, Mum and Dad were at home, but it felt that way anyhow, as if the skulls were right in my bedroom.

By the way, I told Oscar and his pals that it scared me very much when they tricked me to go into the room where they were watching a horror movie. Just because they're older than me doesn't mean they have a right to tease me all the time! They'll have to watch their horror movies by themselves. I don't want to be with them anyway, and if they ask me to come in, I will just refuse. I was afraid when I told him off, Oscar. I guess it's still hard for me when I get angry. Thank you for letting me write to you!

So long,

Emma

P.S. I think it would be a good idea to talk with you a bit further. It's true that I'm older now and I really don't believe that a skull can get into my room. But I'm afraid anyway. Is it all right to come back to you even after all these years?

Brief reply from Majlis

Hello Emma!

Certainly you are welcome to come and talk to me! Your mother phoned me yesterday and asked for an appointment for you. I look forward to seeing you next Thursday after school at three o'clock. The code is 7462.

So long!

Majlis

In the waiting room from Emma

Hello Majlis!

It's five o'clock and I'm still here in your waiting room after our first meeting – I mean after all these years. I asked you if I was allowed to stay in your waiting room until it was time for my basketball practice. But I have to tell you, I was lying a little bit. I wanted to rest for a while and write something that entered my mind. I was not sure whether I should give this letter to you or tear it into pieces or put it into the letter box. In the end, I decided to leave it on the chair in your waiting room.

It was weird to see you again. The room was just as it was four years ago. That also goes for the armchairs and the nice pictures, well, even for your door lock, which was always so difficult to open. The funny thing was that everything was much smaller now compared to what I remember from those days. I was pleased to see you again, but it was also embarrassing.

Sitting here in the waiting room, I have been thinking about what we were talking about today. I think it fits in. But it's strange. I love my mother very much, but sometimes I just can't stand her. It was not like that before. I remember being angry with Daddy and Oscar and the girls at school – but not being mad at Mum. Now I'm quite pissed off with her. Whoops, it scares me even writing those words, "pissed off with Mum". You told me today that now I dare to be angry with her, but that I was very afraid about it before. You know, I think you're right. After all, she was my point of safety, you might say. I wanted to be with her most of the time – even when she became a bit funny and started smelling of wine. To tell you the truth, she smells of wine pretty often. Daddy was okay if

I needed help with my homework or stuff like that. Funny thing to say, but I could be angry with him without being afraid. Sometimes we even had rows but they didn't bother me that much.

Getting cross with Mum was another thing entirely. It was just impossible! Everybody, Daddy, Grandma and you, felt so sorry for her! No, wait, sorry, Majlis, I just made that up. You never said anything like that. But I did think sometimes that you were on Mother's side and that you felt sorry for her. Do you remember when I thought you smelled of alcohol? I got dead scared and thought you were drinking, just like Mum. You had bought a new perfume and it scared me. Suddenly I thought the strange smell that sometimes comes from Mum's mouth was coming from your mouth and skin as well. If only you knew how much I hated that smell – and how it frightened me!

Today, you brought up the idea again about people or characters on the theatre stage. You seem to like that idea, don't you! Earlier, when we met, I finally got to know the Emma-will-die-character. I managed to allow her to act in my "theatre play", you might say. But putting the Mum-will-die-character up on stage: never! It was like a thought that was not even allowed to exist. After all, if that thought had become real I would not have a mother any longer. At least, that was what I kept repeating to myself. So, I put that Mum-will-die-character in some corner of the wardrobe at the theatre. Then I got afraid of those dead people and skulls instead. It's strange, but now that we've been talking about it, it feels a bit easier. And one thing struck me as I was sitting here in your waiting room: maybe it's time that I tell Mum what I think about her drinking thing. I mean, I behave as if I am a little girl who can't talk. But I can talk! It only takes courage . . . Could you help me out on this, please?

See you next week. I just wanted to write and tell you about these things.
Best wishes,

Emma

Chapter 7

We don't look into each other's eyes

Hello Björn!

Today, I've been screaming all day long. Mummy can take me into her arms or leave me in my cot – it just doesn't make any difference. I keep on crying and yelling no matter what. I don't know why. Mummy seems strange today. She's different or maybe I'm different. I don't know. I'm only three months old, and it's hard for me to understand what goes on inside me and around me.

Yesterday, Mum and I were at your place. It wasn't the first time. When we started visiting you I was still in her tummy. In those days, she was so afraid she would never become a good mother. She didn't grasp that I was going to help her! No, no, she saw everything as her responsibility, hers and hers alone. That was how she kept thinking about it. But I was so sweet and lovely when I came out of her tummy that she just couldn't help but love me! Well, you know about those things yourself because we went on visiting you after I was born. I thought it was cosy, lying in her lap, listening to the two of you buzzing words above my head.

But when I was two months old I wanted to take part in your buzzing. You seemed to notice it, because you started talking to me. I did not understand those sounds, but I saw that you were interested in me. Then I thought it was fun to rest in Mum's lap and listen to your voice. Yours is deeper than my mum's. But this morning, everything was so different. The telephone rang. You said something to Mum and left the room. Then you came back and kept on talking. I did not grasp what you were talking about. To me it sounded mostly like bzzzz and mrrrr. But I did notice that Mum had changed! She started sounding as she usually does when we have been giving each other a bad time. Something comes into her voice and she holds me in a different way. This time, it no longer felt as pleasant to lie in her lap in your office as it had before.

When we got back home there was still that same strange thing between Mum and me. She wanted to be nice to me. She thought I was hungry and put me to her breast. But I just couldn't suckle because I was so upset. Then I started to have tummy troubles even though I didn't get any milk. She had to change my diaper. Right afterwards, I had diarrhoea and she had to change my diaper a second time. Now she was clearly annoyed. But I still didn't know what had happened. Have you got any idea? Please answer me as simply as you can. I'm not very old and I don't understand complicated words.

Frida

Reply from Björn

Hello Frida!

Being upset, dirty diapers, a bad stomach, not being able to suckle, Mother annoyed . . . That's not great fun for you or Mum. I will tell you what I think happened. Yesterday the phone rang in my office. I had not turned the ringer off. Silly me! I usually don't forget to do it! When I heard it ringing, I left the room where the three of us were sitting. Well, I guess you were mostly lying in your mother's lap. When I returned from the phone call, your mother was unhappy with me. Sometimes she gets afraid when she gets angry with me. She tends to become sad instead. We were talking about that, she and I. Then I told her that, of course, she must have been quite angry with me. It was only natural. It was not nice of me to leave her alone with you while I went out to answer the phone. But she found it hard to admit that she was angry with me.

Today, when you returned to my office, your mum told me that you had been crying all morning long. Just like you told me yourself in your letter. And then I really got to see for myself what she was talking about! After a few minutes you started screaming at the top of your lungs. You just kept screaming for what seemed an eternity. Your mother did not know what to do. She tried to calm you. She talked to you and tried to nurse you but nothing worked. I guessed she was still angry with me and tense about it. I thought it made her hold you a bit more tightly than usual. I think you noticed all that. But I also think you were angry with your mother too, because you did something to her – can you guess what? When you were screaming you did not look into her eyes. You kept looking everywhere else: through the window, at me, at the bookshelf and up at the ceiling. There was only one place where you never looked: into her eyes. She looked very sad when you looked at everyone and everything but her.

I was thinking that what really makes a mother happy is to see her baby looking into her eyes. Then the whole world feels good to her and to the little one. But what if the baby looks away from her? That cannot be very pleasant, either for the mum or for the baby. What do you think? Am I right that when you are cross with your mum, you don't look into her eyes?

Best wishes from Björn

A slantwise reply from Frida

Hello Björn!

It's strange. Mum and I, we kind of look slantwise at each other. I call it that way when things are bad between us. Most of the time, things are quite good. But sometimes, our eyes are slanting. I cannot tell you who started all this. I am able to notice it when I look at Mum, because I can look at her myself. Sometimes, she doesn't look quite into my eyes! That makes me feel a bit weird. I feel like I might lose her, and you don't want to lose your mum when you are as little as I am. I guess you are right that I do something similar to her. If I am angry with her, I've got something funny buzzing around inside me. This something tells me not to look into her eyes. So I get "on the slant" with her.

Why don't I want to look into my mother's eyes when I am annoyed with her? Once I really did try to look at her even though I was annoyed. I thought she looked so scary, like a ghost. Maybe she only looked that way in unreality. But it's not easy for me to distinguish reality from unreality. I have been living outside my mum's body for only three months now. Before that, I lived inside her all of the time but I can't remember much of it. Today, things are different. Life outside Mummy's tummy is more interesting but sometimes it is scarier. It is more interesting because Mum and I can have a great time. Sometimes when she looks at me, I can see all that love glowing from her eyes. Can you imagine being so little and already having someone who is in love with you?

But then there is the scary part, too, when she doesn't look into my eyes and when I don't look into her eyes. This happens when we are "on the slant" with each other, I mean, we're not such good friends. That's not fun! Could you help us so that we are able to look into each other's eyes even when we are annoyed with each other? But now I can't write any more. Mummy just gave me my evening meal from her breast. Everything feels fuzzy and my eyes are closing.

Goodnight from Frida

Goodnight from Björn

Dear Frida!

It's nine o'clock in the evening and I guess you are asleep while I am thinking of you. "On the slant with each other" – that was a good expression. I did notice that Mum got annoyed with me about the phone call incident. I also noticed that when I came back into the room she did not look into my eyes either. Her eyes moved around to everything but me. I think I even asked her, "Hello, are you cross with me, could we have some contact!?" But no, there was not much contact in the beginning. It was as if she and I were on the slant with each other.

When the two of you returned to my office for the next session the day afterwards, Mum told me that you had been very troublesome. I got this idea: if Mum couldn't look at me when she was annoyed with me, how could she look at you? After a while, I got the answer to my question. When you started screaming in my office, she was looking away from you – and you looked away from her. It was sad to see how both of you were on the slant with each other, as you call it. But I kept on talking to both of you. You might say that I went right into the heart of matters instead of staying slantwise with Mum and you. I told your mother that I felt quite sure that your screaming and other upsets had something to do with her anger with me the day before – and that you probably noticed that she had become different. She held you in her arms in a different way from what you're used to. I also guess her voice changed. Above all, she didn't look into your eyes. That was plain to see.

I also talked to you about what I thought had happened the day before and this morning. The phone rang, Mum felt I had abandoned her, she got angry with me and then you had that terrible morning afterwards. Things just got worse, and you kept screaming to the point where Mum felt like she would go deaf! But when you and I met again, I kept looking at you all the time. I also talked to you a lot and told you how I thought you had felt about all these things. You noticed my face and my bzzzz and mrrrr sounds, as you call them. In the end, you just could not resist looking at me. You might not remember it, but in the end you became quite curious about me and to top it all off you gave me a wonderful smile. Can we say that all's well that ends well? Not quite, because Mum and you need to deal with this habit of going on the slant with each other. And Mum and I need to deal with the next situation when she gets angry with me. After all, looking at someone slantwise is not a good way to make someone understand that you are cross with him. We will have to talk about these matters later. But now it is about time even for a grown-up fellow like me to go to bed.

Goodnight, Frida.

Björn

Chapter 8

My head is a mess

Hi Noah!

First of all, congratulations on your birthday! Ten years – not bad! I hope you will have a nice day with breakfast in bed and many gifts from Mum, Dad and your little sister. I also hope that your birthday party next Saturday will be great fun. I remember last year when you and I were talking about your party. You told me you also wanted to invite your classmate Ken, though you weren't sure about it. When we met a few days after the party, you just strode right into my office and shouted, "You psycho nerd!" You said my loo was stinking. I understood nothing, because you had been looking forward to your party and I didn't know what had been going on. Then you told me. When you had invited the boys in your class, Ken had called you "ADHD freak" and told you he wanted nothing to do with your party.

After hesitating for a while you told me that you had reacted the way you sometimes do – you punched Ken on the nose. Some teachers came along and held you while he wiped off the blood running from his nose. As is usual, you got the blame for everything. So it was, even if you thought that Ken had started it all. And you, well, you just couldn't explain how you felt when he called you an ADHD freak. When you told me about it I suggested that you had probably felt hurt. You just shrugged your shoulders and said, "I didn't get hurt – check it out, I have no blood anywhere. Ken was the one who got hurt, not me! Wow! There was blood pouring from his nose!" Then I told you that a person can feel hurt in different ways: "You can bleed blood and you can bleed feelings." You cut me off with, "That's just psycho talk."

Anyway, that was last year. Now it's time to celebrate your tenth birthday. The other day you told me that from now on you'll have two digits in your age. I remember myself when I had my tenth birthday. I thought this would be the last time in my life that another digit was added to my years. In those days nobody imagined that a person might reach one hundred years of age. The night before my tenth birthday I was quite sad, but I didn't tell anybody. When you are a boy you don't talk very much about such things. You keep them to yourself. I have a hunch that you know what I mean.

Now I got lost in my own thoughts. As I told you, I wish you a happy birthday and a nice party. I also hope that you'll get some really nice birthday gifts. See you soon! By the way, is Ken coming to your party this year?

Regards,

Björn

Reply from Noah

Hello Björn!

Thanks for your letter. It was cool hearing from you. For my birthday, I got a PlayStation from Mum and Dad. It was the latest version. Exactly the one I wanted! Wow, I really got excited! The next problem is to get them to allow me to stay up late at night. Otherwise I won't have a chance to master all the levels. "Level" is that thing which you did not know anything about when it comes to these games. Remember when we talked about it? It means that someone can be good in different ways in the game. I have already reached level six. I don't want to boast about it, but to tell you the truth you wouldn't stand a chance against me!

Ken is not coming to my party. I'm not going to invite him because he might tease me again and I don't want that to happen. It's not because I'd beat him up. I've stopped doing things like that. It's more because Ken is strong in what he says and I get damned sad when he insults me. You've been nagging me and wanting me to talk about how I often feel sad. I always say it's nothing but the other day something strange happened. Mum asked me if I was going to invite Ken to my party. I went dead silent. She asked me why I was rubbing my eyes. I hadn't even noticed! Then she stroked my head and said, "I guess you've got some tears in your eyes today, Noah."

At first I felt annoyed with her, but then I noticed how kind she sounded. So I checked it out. There really were some tears on my cheek. I kept thinking about it, that other way, the "inwards-way" as I call it. She was right; I did get sad when she asked me about Ken. I told Mum about it, and she patted my cheek and gave me a muffin. The muffin was okay.

As I told you, I got a PlayStation from Mum and Dad. My little sister gave me a rock 'n' roll CD. Do you remember when we talked about that song by Per Gessle, the song that says "all my feelings come rushing at the same time"? If you don't know who Per is, I can tell you that he is the leading guy in Roxette, one of the world's most famous rock 'n' roll groups. Wonder if I'll become a musician one day. I really don't know. Constructing PlayStations would be fun too. Good I don't have to decide yet, isn't it! I brought my MP3 player to your place so we could listen to the tune together. You told me it was not easy when one's feelings come rushing all at the same time. I thought you were really stupid when you said that. I just wanted you to listen to the song, but no, no, you just couldn't stop yourself from psycho-babbling like you always do!

Dad is going to help me read the manual for the PlayStation. The next chapter is called, and I hope I spell it correctly now, "How to Become Invincible". Dad explained this hard word to me. He told me it means that a player becomes so skilful in a game that nobody can beat him. How I would love to be invincible, you'd better believe it!

Have a nice day,
Regards from Noah

The invincible Noah – reply from Björn

Hello again Noah!

Invincible. Yes, you did spell it correctly. I checked it myself. Strange word – I would not have known it myself when I was ten. Well, I guess everyone wants to win at games and no one wants to be teased. You were wise to choose not to invite Ken to your party. After all, he has been teasing you and all your feelings might have come rushing again, all at the same time, just like in that song. Sometimes, things get messy and this can happen even when a lot of nice feelings come rushing. For example, you like your schoolmate Sophie very much. But when we talk about her, things get troublesome for you. It is as if there is a flood inside your head. Then all the loves, if we may put it that way, come rushing all at the same time. This is when you say you feel like your head is a mess.

Do you remember when we spoke about that mess for the first time? Once you made up a game. You asked me to make a cootie, that thing made out of a sheet of paper that you fold a few times and then you put colours on every corner of it. You told me to write secret messages on every flap of the cootie. You dictated the secret messages. Then I was supposed to point at a coloured flap and you would open it. You did so and I read out loud what had been written there – all according to your orders. The line went as follows: "Kiss and hug the wall." You cried out, "Do it!" But instead I kept asking what you were thinking when you asked me to write "kiss" on that flap of the paper. You pretended to ignore my question and kept ordering me, "Kiss the wall, do it now, Björn!" I was wondering aloud how a person might feel if he is asked to kiss a wall. What would people think if I went up to the wall and started kissing it? Would they tease me? I told you about all these thoughts of mine so you could also hear them. Suddenly, you told me that your sister teases you and calls you her "ADHD brother". Just as suddenly you told me that you must go to the loo. And off you went.

When you returned, I told you I had been thinking about something. It must be awful being teased about having ADHD. I guessed you had been harassed by your sister, and now you wanted to harass me by forcing me to kiss the wall. And then, all those feelings about Sophie. I think you would like to kiss her. But you have told me that she does not care about you and does not seem interested in kissing you. I wonder how such things feel inside you. Does it feel like kissing a wall? I guess all these thoughts make your feelings come rushing into your head.

When I had talked to you about these things, you looked very serious and told me, "My head is just a mess." I was moved and told you, "Maybe we could clear up that mess together." You stretched out your hands a little and suddenly got shy. You mumbled something about your dirty fingers and nails and then you became silent. I have noticed many times that when you turn silent it means that you are thinking about what we have been talking about.

Good luck with your levels!
Björn

Reply from Noah

Hello Björn!

Today Ken bullied me again. As usual, he called me an ADHD freak. Then he made fun of me for seeing a psychologist. He sneered at me when he said those things. I felt so angry that it was hard not to beat him up again. I wondered how he knew about me seeing a psycho. I haven't told anybody about it! At first I thought you had been gossiping, but that didn't make any sense. You wouldn't do a thing like that. Marie, who is an after-school care leader at my school and who I like very much, asked me, "Why don't you tell Ken why you see a psychologist, Noah?" At first I just wanted to die on the spot, it was so embarrassing. But then I thought what the heck and I did it. I just didn't know how to start. Then suddenly, it was as if I was hearing that song about the feelings inside my head!

This is what I told Ken: "Imagine that your head is just a mess. You get it?" He did, believe it or not. Then I told him that's how my life is sometimes. I explained to him that I need to see a psychologist to bring

My head is a mess 57

some order into that mess. I sort of lost him there, so I knew I had to explain myself better. So I put some pebbles in my hand. He got dead scared thinking I was going to throw them at him.

"Take it easy," I told Ken. "I just want to show you something. This is how things are in my head sometimes." I threw all the pebbles up in the air and they all fell to the ground. It was just a mess. "Could you put all these pebbles in order, just like they were in my hand before?" "Of course not," he said and he shook his head and shrugged his shoulders.

"Now I'll put the pebbles into order," I told Ken. I picked them up and tried to put them in my hand the same way they were before. Of course, that was impossible but I managed so-so. "What's that got to do with a psychologist?" Ken asked me. At first, I thought he was superstupid because he didn't get it. But then I remembered that it took me a long time to grasp these things myself. So I told him I see a psycho to sort things out in my head. "It's kind of similar to what I was doing with the pebbles!" Once again, Ken shrugged his shoulders and asked me if we could play football instead.

I'm not sure that Ken really got it with the pebbles. But I was happy anyway. At first I had the idea of beating him up. When Marie asked me to tell him why I come to see you, she sounded friendly. I guess that's why I did what she said. I felt really smart about being able to make that thing up with the pebbles. But now I don't have time to explain more about that stuff. I am going to play with my PlayStation again. If I make another round, I'll reach level seven. The problem is that Mum and Dad think that I'm asleep already. I've got to be as quiet as a mouse.

Goodnight!

Noah

P.S. When I got tired of all those levels, I checked something out on my PC. Do you know there are things called emoticons? They are tiny little faces that show what your feelings are like. Well, I guess you're too old to know about things like that. When you're writing on your PC, you can type some of them yourself! Or, if you want to see more of them, just google on the Internet! I think that's pretty cool. The simplest way is to do like this: when you press : and) at the same time, you get this one: ☺. Anyone can see that the guy is happy. Or, if you press : and (you get the opposite face: ☹. Pretty grumpy, isn't he? My problem is that when I feel really bad, it seems like somebody took all the emoticons of the world and made an omelette out of them. But when I think about what I did with the pebbles and Ken, I feel very cool and satisfied. Then I can see that the omelette has many kinds of pebbles in it, even if I'm not so sure I'd like to eat an omelette made of pebbles! You could also put it this way: all the pebbles, all the feelings, come rushing, not at the same time but one after the other. Then I don't get so confused and embarrassed. That's good.

Chapter 9

Restless and ruthless – or just rootless?

Mother!

You must hurry and come along with us! I cannot wait any longer. Everybody is leaving tomorrow night. If my camel driver Ankh-What is right about the speed of his trusty creature of the land, you will receive this letter tonight. Reply immediately! What would people say if I told them that I must wait until my mother has answered whether or not she wants to join us to go to the Promised Land? They have already called me a troublemaker. I do not want to be called, in addition, a mama's boy.

I cannot stand to be in Egypt any longer. The oppression, the humiliation, the lack of liberty, everything gets on my nerves. All the time we meet these hateful glances, as soon as we achieve something good. The only time they smile at us is when we die. Worst of all is that something is insidiously rotting the very soul of my people. They are becoming lazy and comfortable. "I don't mind a little lack of liberty as long there's food on my table . . ." That's what one of us told me the other day. As usual I got very angry and was on the verge of slapping him in the face. The man mumbled something in apology and just disappeared. People are afraid of my hot temper.

Am I a troublemaker? What is your opinion, Mother? You, who have known me all my life? It doesn't make a person a troublemaker just because he thinks people are wrong, does it? But this is what they call me. Yes, I tend to get angry easily. My mind whirls into a fury, like the desert wind, when something makes me upset. "You are so moralistic that you tend to become amoral," says my sister Miriam. "Your quarrel with that man who preferred food to freedom – that's a good example!" Then I got angry with her as well. But she insisted and told me there was another example. She looked around anxiously. Then I understood what she was hinting at. You know as well, but I cannot write it. If Pharaoh's men were to know what I have done, they would bury me alive.

Come along on our great journey, Mother! You and I have not always been on good terms, and our lives have taken different directions. But now you are old and live alone since Father passed away. It will be a brief journey across the Red Sea, and then through the desert towards the land which is supposed to be filled with milk and honey. I promise to build you the most exclusive hut that you have ever seen. Please answer yes!

Warmest love from your son,

Moses

A letter from Moses's mother

Dear Son!

My answer can be found already in your letter: I am old and I have been through many things in my life. Ever since your father died, something has been slowly trickling out of me. I do not know if it is my appetite to live or my belief in the future. And you know that I have never got over your little brother's death, the boy without a name. When he was killed your father tried to comfort me by making me inhale the perfume of the lotus flower. We decided to call him Lotus Flower. To this very day I cannot stand the scent of it at the marketplace and I have to run away immediately.

But you, Moses, you made it. I was young and alert and everything was under my control – at least that was how I felt about life then. You really take after your mother! But even back then I was afraid that life would turn into a nightmare. I was pregnant when Pharaoh's order was issued that every newborn boy of our people was to be murdered. There was a time when I thought I was going to lose you before you even left my womb. One night, you were completely motionless inside me. You, always kicking about and making me feel as if there were some sea wind blowing inside my belly! Now, there was no sign of life whatsoever. I asked the midwife Sifra if the foetus could die out of a mother's fear. But she put her head on my belly and smiled reassuringly, "No danger at all – he's swimming about inside. Things will be alright!" I thought that if you were to be born alive I would take it as a divine sign and do everything possible to save your life. I promised to do so even though it might mean that I was going to lose you to someone else. The night you were born, something else dawned on me: the idea to make a basket and put it in that current of life and death, the great river Nile.

The next day, you were born. You were a strong and happy baby, and I started immediately to make a little basket out of reeds that I had gathered by the Nile. Your father and the midwife told me I was foolish. They said, "If the crocodiles don't swallow him, some robbers will surely grab him and sell him to Nubian slave traders." But I did not listen to them. I made the basket quite narrow and in the shape of an agave leaf. That way it would float easily into the midst of the river and neither crocodiles nor robbers would be able to snatch you. Further down the river, I knew there was a bend. I hoped you would be stranded there. "Either Pharaoh's people will discover him and then he might make it, or . . ." I could not imagine another outcome.

I nursed you from my frightened breasts. Sifra had a magic spell she had learnt from her mother. It seemed to work wonders because I had a lot of milk and you grew rapidly. But when you were three months old, I could no longer hide you. That was when I carried out my plan. Your father and Sifra went down to the river, where they found the basket, which I had hidden among the reeds. I stayed at home, because I was not strong enough to leave you by the river. Your father placed an amulet on your chest. In the end he pushed the basket out on the river. The last sound they heard from you was some kind of funny giggling. This is what he told me when they got back home. I took that as a good sign.

You know the rest of the story. Your sister Miriam ran to the Pharaoh's palace to spy. My plan worked! The princess picked you up out of the river bank. Miriam tricked the princess to arrange a nurse for you. They did not tell her that the nurse was me, your own mother! Perhaps the princess intuited who I was, though she did not reveal anything. I know she was a good person.

But I have never told you I how I felt inside about all these trials and tribulations. At first when I was pregnant, I felt as if you had perished inside of me. Then Sifra reassured me that you were alive. Then I gave birth to you. Briefly thereafter, I had to desert you by the river. I had the good fortune to be near you once again for some time as your nurse and breathe in the lovely scent of your little hands. In the end, I had to bring you back to the royal court. Everybody told me, "Rejoice! You are nursing a boy who will become a prince one day." But there were so many heavy thoughts when I put you to bed. "Tomorrow they might come and get him. Perhaps this is my last night with him." I weaned you as slowly as possible, but in the end I had to let you go. I could not look at you when you were chuckling, and I could not rejoice when I saw how quickly you had grown thanks to my milk. You were only lent to me! Dark and cold winds run through my mind even today whenever I think of this time in my life. When your little brother was born I did not have the strength to make such great schemes any more. They just took him. I never saw him again.

Sometimes, I think I should have thrown myself with him into the Nile River, but your father told me not to think that way. Now I am old and life has not been easy. You are young and eager to get out of Egypt and to journey to the Promised Land. Leave this country now and do it with my blessing! But leave without me.

Wishing you good fortune and happiness,
Your mother

Moses got his mother's letter only after he had led his people across the Red Sea. The next letter was written many years later. It was written to Moses by his son Gershom. His son is now a young man and his father's life is coming to an end after forty years of wandering in the desert.

A letter from Gershom, Moses's son, to his father

Dear Father!

I am out in the desert on a spy mission. Once again you have ordered me to spy on our numerous enemies, who are going to attack us any day now. Maybe you are right that they want to destroy us – I do not really know. This time, my mission will last longer than expected. There will be many lonely nights by the campfire before I may return to my wife and to our newborn twins.

Being on this mission gives me unexpected time for thinking. There are so many stories about you and I often wonder if they are true. Is it true that you sailed on the Nile River in a reed basket? Did Pharaoh's daughter really pick you up and raise you? Is it true that manna rained down from heaven when people were revolting against you because they did not get any meat? All these questions have been troubling me ever since I was a boy. There are other questions as well. They have always scared me and I wonder whether I should ask you or not. After all, you can be rather stern and your temper is so unpredictable.

When we were small, my siblings and I used to wonder and make jokes about you. "Father is restless, or is he ruthless, or is he *both* restless and ruthless?" We used to giggle a lot and thought it was fun to say such things about you. But we would never have dared to say them aloud to you! People used to think you were patient, but we knew you could get angry quite easily. If you were as patient as people thought you were, why did you kill an Egyptian when you were young? Can one really call a person patient if he kills someone out of sheer anger?

As I see the campfire slowly going out, I keep thinking of you. The more I think, the more puzzled I become. You are a great leader, but you have got that severe stuttering; you interpret the law, but when you are bad-tempered you act as if you were an outlaw. I am old enough not to believe that there is an answer to every question. At least there is not always an easy answer. I also know that we human beings are not easy to understand. I love you with all your peculiarities – and I feel sorry for you. You brought us out from slavery in Egypt, but you were not permitted to bring us into the Promised Land. And all of this just because you made a little amendment in the order of God! You were supposed to speak to the rock in order to get water for us. Instead, you hit it with your stick. You wanted to act as a magician and in that way increase people's respect for you. But God is even sterner than you and gave you a severe punishment: you will never enter the Promised Land.

My sheet of papyrus is running out and the campfire has gone out completely. I wonder if you are willing to speak with me about those matters. Some day.

Your son,

Gershom

Reply from a father to his son

My dear son!

I am a shy man and I find it difficult to talk. Long conversations just make me feel restless. I prefer to write to you instead of waiting until you come home and we could talk. I will tell you about a dream that keeps coming back ever since I was a young man in Pharaoh's court. In that dream I run. I am tired and thirsty. On a pathway, I can see a house in front of me and I get the idea that inside this house I will find peace at last. I feel convinced that someone will welcome me in there, and give me food and shelter. I also hear happy voices and I catch the glimpse of a woman. But every time I have this dream the door is locked. Sometimes, there is not even a door but instead I just run into the wall. I tend to wake up from that dream sweaty and scared, but also relieved that it was just a dream.

Many years ago I asked the chief interpreter of dreams in Pharaoh's court what might be the meaning of my recurrent dream. I was still a young man and even more impatient than today, so I did not pay much attention to his answer. He seemed uncomfortable and said, "The dream is about you and your mother, the Hebrew." I got scared and asked, "Why do you think my mother is a Hebrew woman?" He responded, "I know more things than you believe." Of course, I got scared when he spoke like that, but he looked friendly and continued: "In your dream you are running towards your mother. But she does not receive you. You run after her but every time you fail. It is as if you cannot reach her or perhaps she does not have the strength to console you. Both interpretations are possible." I understood nothing of it and left him sitting there with all his Egyptian wisdom.

Shortly after our exodus from Egypt, I received a letter from my mother, your grandmother. In this letter she explained why she did not want to join me on the journey to the Promised Land. In those days, our people lived in constant terror. The greatest happiness that could be bestowed upon a mother, to deliver a healthy child, had been turned into a nightmare: newborn children were to be taken away from their mothers, to be killed by Pharaoh's soldiers.

The rest of my story you have heard many times: about how your brave grandmother put me in a reed basket in the Nile River and how Pharaoh's daughter took care of me. You have also heard how my sister Miriam arranged for my mother to be allowed to nurse me. As you now understand, all these stories are true. But there is one thing that you do not know, and neither did I at the time it happened. I have only known it since I read your grandmother's letter about how she was feeling in those days. The pain she experienced never left her. Every time she looked at me, all her sorrows invaded her.

When I began to catch some glimpse of those matters, I also started to understand Pharaoh's chief interpreter. In the dream I never reached the house. In reality, I never seemed to reach my mother. She was a refined, strong and conscientious woman. She even had a stern beauty. But did I ever reach her in the way that I wanted to reach the house in my dream? I do not believe so. I am not quite certain in what ways all this is connected with your questions about my impatience and sternness. You are right. I tend to flare up easily without considering matters in advance. Much too often I speak to my brothers and sisters in a relentless or even rude manner. Probably I am not as stern or mean as I seem. No, it is rather as if I never reach my own house. I never reach that kind of stillness and peace inside of me that I notice in other people. It is as if I am standing outside myself and knocking on the door in order to be let in – into myself. But the door is locked and I run away in anger and disappointment. When you and your sister made fun of me, whispering, "Father is restless and ruthless", you were right. What you might have added, but which I myself did not understand at that time, was that I am also a rootless man. Not only because I once left my home country Egypt and headed for an unknown faraway land. No, there is also a rootlessness inside of me. It is as if some cords once were cut off inside of me, and I am still struggling to tie them together again.

Finally, here is what I would like to tell you about the story of the rock and the water. No, I did not intend to act as a magician when I hit the rock. I hit it because I was not patient enough for the water to come running through the rock. When eventually that water came gushing out, I felt relieved, that kind of relief that is so rarely bestowed upon me. The cruel punishment, that I would never be allowed to enter the Promised Land, I take as a punishment for my lack of patience. I always recognize myself from that dream whenever I stand upon the mountain and I see in the far distance the land of milk and honey. All in all, I can console myself in the knowledge that I have had a good life. It could have ended in the jaws of a crocodile or in Pharaoh's prison. To be sure, it will end in a desert. But I rejoice when I realize that this desert holds the promise of a land for my people. It is also a desert where I came to know many wonderful persons, including you, my son.

Your father,

Moses

Chapter 10

Letter from the volcano

Konichiwa Björn!

U like this pic from Japan? Studying Japanese before deciding what to do for the rest of my life. Long time no see. Took Shinkansen train yesterday from Tokyo (where I'm studying) to Kyoto, passing Fuji Mountain. Wow! Last night a dream about a volcano made me think of one time when you and I talked about a volcano. Sure was a long time ago!

Hope all is well over there in your part of the world!

Best regards – if you remember me!

Linda

Reply from Björn

Konichiwa Linda!

"Arigato" or thank you for your e-mail and photo of Fuji. I know only five words in Japanese, but I sure know that Fuji is a fabulous mountain! Of course, I remember you, though almost a decade has passed. You were around ten years old at that time. Just like you wrote, "Long time no see", but inside of me it doesn't feel that long ago. We worked together for some years, and all those meetings have come together into a kind of photo album in my head. It's a bit like with old friends – you don't forget them, do you?

I remember that you and I got to know each other a week or two after your parents phoned me. They wanted an appointment because they were concerned about you. When we met they told me they thought you were almost too diligent at school. "No problem to get Linda to do her homework, never any mischief or emotional outbursts," they told me. They had a feeling that your classmates harassed you, but you didn't want to tell them about it. In those days you were nine years old. Today, you're twice as old. What about you? How much do you remember from the days we worked together?

Warm regards,

Björn

From Linda

Hello Björn!

Today I've got more spare time, so you'll get a more extensive e-mail! You asked me what I remember. Well, I recall how afraid I was at first and how I was just sitting there, tense and withdrawn, in your office. I couldn't think of anything to say and I wondered how we were supposed to talk to each other. But we finally got started and managed to work together after all. I think it had something to do with that game in the schoolyard: Monkey in the Middle. I don't remember much more than this right now. Perhaps you remember. So long now, I've got to go to my Japanese class. Sorry I didn't have more time for this e-mail after all. I guess I'm still a time optimist, always on the verge of being late . . .

Linda

Björn replies

Hello again Linda!

I remember a lot, because I used to take notes after our meetings. Yes, the very first time we met we talked about that Monkey in the Middle game. You told me how you were playing it with your classmates and they made you be the monkey. The "middle" was a kind of prison. You could get out of it only if you caught the ball they threw to you. But they ganged up and threw it so you couldn't catch it. You wanted to get out of the middle. But your classmates wouldn't allow you to move until you caught the ball, which they made impossible for you. "Those are the rules!" they claimed. You told me that actually they didn't want you to take part in the game at all. You added, "To tell you the truth, sometimes I do the same sort of thing when I don't want some certain person to play in a game."

So, quite often you felt that your classmates were not nice to you. But you also admitted that sometimes you did something similar to a girl you didn't like. Most of all, I kept thinking about how you might be feeling as you stood there, not wanting to be the monkey in the middle. You told me it was icy and slippery when you were standing in the middle, and in my mind's eye I saw that icy patch. Suddenly I felt sad. It was like a video was running inside my head. I saw a girl who couldn't catch the ball and who tried to leave the middle of the circle. But she just couldn't do it and so she stayed a monkey. That monkey is the character who is rejected – she's the loser. You assured me that the game has rules. I replied that, of course, the game has rules, but those rules just don't work when classmates gang up together and decide to be nasty.

I thought you felt inside and outside at the same time. You were inside the monkey's circle, but I thought it would be more appropriate to call it a cage. And you were also feeling outside the circle of your classmates. I really felt sorry for you and thought your classmates were no good friends. But then something happened; as we began working together I noticed that there were times I felt excluded by *you*. Sometimes I even felt a bit silly sitting with you. I felt like I was stuck in the monkey area and was not allowed to come over and join you. These were some of the things that happened when you visited me some years ago. Memories tend to come back to my mind, as you notice. I am glad that you wrote to me. I hope sushi and all the other exciting things in Japan will help you to find out what you want to do with your life!

Keep well over there,

Björn

Linda in Stockholm

Hello Björn!

I arrived in Stockholm a few days ago for a short visit. It hurts a bit to read your letter, I must admit. It's true that I was a rather lonely and unhappy girl back in those days. Today I feel better, though life isn't perfect. I have a boyfriend and I'm very fond of him. We have kind of the same interests. He likes sushi too, which is always an advantage.

I'm going to return to Japan in two weeks. I want to remain there another year before deciding what to study in the future. Can you believe that the ambitious and diligent Linda is going to work in Japan just for the fun of it? It doesn't seem impossible to get a temporary job here, like babysitting or bartending. I guess my parents are going to blow their tops when they find out about it, but that's their problem and not mine! After all, I've just turned eighteen so I've come of age. What did you think about my volcano dream? You didn't comment on it. Sometimes I feel I understand why that dream keeps coming back, and sometimes I understand nothing at all. Have you got any idea? Do write to me if you understand it!

Regards,

Linda

Reply from Björn

Hello again Linda!

I think I've found a clue. I've looked at my notes from one of our meetings, one that took place after the Easter holidays. At that time we had known each other for more than a year, and you were ten years old by then. When you entered my office, you made a drawing with your left hand. Since you are right-handed, you were actually using your "wrong" hand. From what I could see, it looked a bit awkward. You moved to block me from seeing it. It was obvious that you were not going to show it to me. You seemed alone and sad. Once again, I felt excluded by you because, of course, I wanted to see your drawing but you wouldn't let me.

Suddenly you said in an agitated tone of voice, "Why don't they ever give the names of animals acting in movies? Some kids took part in a theatre play but they didn't get paid much. Then there was an adult actor just dragging a box. He got paid much more than the kids!"

I said to you, "I wonder if this is how you were feeling when I took my Easter break and you couldn't see me? Maybe you felt just like the children and the animals you told me about. I'm an adult so I decided when to take a break. But you're a child and must follow what I decided to do." As a matter of fact, when this incident with the left-handed drawing took place, I had just taken my Easter break and I thought that perhaps you had been missing our meetings.

You didn't buy that idea at all! You just kept on drawing without saying a word. I started feeling more and more uncomfortable and restless. After a while I began to feel guilty because my thoughts were wandering away from you. Instead, I started wondering about how I could climb the ladder to a greater success in my profession. It was embarrassing! But then I started thinking. Perhaps I got greedy for more recognition because I found it painful not to understand what you were feeling and what you were thinking about. On top of it all, I was not allowed to see your drawing. It was as if I were thinking, "Okay, fine, just let her sit there and pretend to be neither little nor excluded. As for me, I'm going to make a big name for myself – just wait and see!"

All these things were on my mind, but I didn't tell you about them. What I did tell you was this: "It's often the case that some people get to decide, whereas others just have to follow their decision. Some people are excluded, like me in this situation right now, because I'm not able to see what you are drawing. Others, like you in this case, remain at the centre of the action and know everything about what is going on there."

You hummed something I don't remember. And then you said something I didn't expect: "I'm thinking about my little sister. It's her birthday in two weeks . . . I remember a drawing I made once." You took out a drawing from your box. Two children are being dragged along by an adult. You said with some hesitation, "My sister is the smallest person in the family – but though she's not as big as I am she takes up ever so much space at home." You looked quite serious, even sad, at that point. I am attaching a copy of your drawing.

So long,

Björn

70 Letter from the volcano

Could we meet, Björn?

Hi again Björn!

Thanks for the drawing. When I saw it I got an idea. Couldn't we meet now before I go back to Japan? I'm free next week on Monday or Tuesday before my departure ... Can you make it?

Linda

Reply from Björn

Hello Linda!

Good idea! I hadn't understood that you were still in town. You're welcome to come to my office on Monday at one o'clock. You know the address – it's the same as before but the code has been changed to 8573.

Björn

We meet

This dialogue took place during our meeting, the following Monday.

Björn: Here is the drawing with the adults dragging along two children. Some years have indeed passed since you made that one!

Linda: I remember it . . . I guess that was how I felt most of the time in those days.

Björn: Look here! Here's another drawing you made some months later. Do you recall it?

Linda: Well, I don't know ... Look! I have written two strange words there. PAKLARASA and PETUNUS. I wonder what those words meant.

Björn: They are secret! That was what you told me when you wrote them! And I responded that secret words can't be understood by anyone who doesn't know the code.

Linda: My sister and I had a secret alphabet. We used to make drawings instead of letters. For example, we drew a rainbow instead of the letter R. My classmates also had secret alphabets.

Björn: Yes, we were talking about how a person might feel if she doesn't know anything about this secret alphabet. Paklarasa and Petunus were incomprehensible – and that was just the point. When you showed them to me, I felt both excluded and stupid because I didn't understand their meaning at all. I guess that was how you felt with your classmates.

Linda: Do you see here, I also made some special letters! Now I remember. The letter U in Petunus was a secret sign which meant "uruption". I guess spelling wasn't my cup of tea in those days. I actually meant eruption. Do you see that letter? It actually looks like a volcano. The other U looks like a snake. Eruption – you can use it for volcano but also for human beings.

Björn: That is what I told you at that time. But you kept assuring me that you would never have an outbreak or eruption only because your classmates had a secret alphabet!

Linda: Eruption from volcanoes, eruption from feelings. I guess I was just as afraid of volcanoes as of feelings. I am beginning to understand why I dreamt about that volcano which I mentioned in my first e-mail to you from Japan. I don't think it happened only because I was passing Mount Fuji.

Björn: I'd like to hear about that. But first I'd just like to recall another drawing. When you made it you told me it was a nose. But I kept thinking it looked like a volcanic eruption.

Linda: It seems to be an angry drawing. Look! I have written "arj [arg] person" (angry person) under the flames of the volcano. Once again, spelling wasn't my favourite subject ...

Björn: You made this drawing once when you were angry with me, but you didn't want to admit it. You were quite angry with other people, too, like your parents, your sister and your classmates. But you didn't dare to show these people how angry you were. I think you were afraid that if you expressed your anger, they would exclude you and isolate you and make you be the monkey trapped in the middle.

Linda: That's what I've been thinking about when it comes to my volcano dream. I guess that when I saw old Mount Fuji out there in the Japanese landscape I was reminded of another volcano: one that had started rumbling inside of me! Let me explain to you: the day before my dream, I had been on Skype with my boyfriend back home in Sweden. I wanted him to visit me in Japan, because I missed him so much and wanted to see him.

	But he just kept on talking about his exams before summer break and that he was going to a party with some friends. Suddenly I heard a girl laughing in the background. I got jealous but I didn't ask him who she was. I was afraid he was going to tease me about it. Or, even worse, that he had got another girlfriend . . .
Björn:	So you made a volcano dream instead.
Linda:	Yes, that was clever of me, wasn't it? Clever but not really helpful! I need to dare to express what I feel, just like you were talking about. Well, I did talk to him about it when I returned to Sweden, but I was too cautious with him! Next time I think I'll have a little eruption against him at once, so he'll understand that I don't want to be treated that way . . . Well, it's about time for me to go now. Thank you for seeing me again before I go back to Japan.
Björn:	Thank you! I'm glad you could come by so that we could talk a little more about what we had been writing in our letters.
Linda:	Gozaimazda. In case you don't know, it means "thank you very much" in Japanese.

Chapter 11

That tingling feeling

Dear Diary!

How strange! My body keeps tingling and I almost feel dizzy. I think about *him* all the time, his red hair and his warm, hearty laughter. I long to get out and see him and run through the woods with him instead of hanging around at home at Matt's Fort. I feel so shut in and bored. I used to like being in my little corner with my leatherwork, pine cones and pebbles. Now everything's just lying there abandoned. All the people who live together with me here at the fort, my parents and my father's robber band, probably notice that I've changed. Yesterday I dropped my plate into the soup tureen. The day before yesterday, I had forgotten that it was my turn to bring in wood for the fireplace. My father, Matt, keeps pacing about and his face is black as thunder. I don't like it when he is in a bad mood. But I don't care. Well, yes, I do care actually, but I just have to get out into that forest again. What if *he* is there! I just have to check it out. Oh, I am so curious to know more about him!

It all started when we had a jumping contest to and fro across Hell's Gap. We kept goading each other on, him and me. It was just a long and tedious competition. Back then I thought he was stupid, ugly and irritating. I kept staring at that ridiculous gap he had up there between his teeth. But now . . . I don't recognize myself. When I was younger, a couple of weeks ago, I went to the forest all the time to get to know what's so beautiful and creepy about it. I mean, wading in the brook and swimming in the river and climbing the mossy boulders and watching out for all the trolls and things like that. But now I want to go there to see if he's there as well. And today, I think that the gap between his front teeth is adorable – well, perhaps not adorable, but, yes, to be honest, adorable. And then I wonder how it would feel if I touched it with my little finger.

I've lived in this forest all my life. My mother, Lovis, told me that while she was giving birth to me there was a great thunderstorm and the entire Matt's Fort was split in two. That was how Hell's Gap was created.

It runs right through the fort and that's why they've been warning me about it all my life. They've told me that a lot of terrible things could happen to a person if she got near it, like toes could start growing out of her stomach or she could give birth to misshapen babies.

I don't even recall all the things that they told me in order to frighten me about Hell's Gap. I never thought that I would be able to jump across it. Never in my life! But when I saw *him* standing there on the other side of the Gap, looking at me with a teasing smile, I could not resist doing it. I don't recall whether it was me or him who was the first one to jump. Perhaps we decided to jump at the same time. These things actually don't matter very much once you stop competing with each other. Once we got started, we just kept jumping to and fro, again and again.

I think that was the first time I experienced that tingling feeling. It was as if I had never known that it existed at all. Well, of course, I can have some sort of tingling feelings when spring is approaching and I just have to give that great spring yell of mine. Or when I jump into the cold water of the brook or run into the forest as fast as I can. Oh, yes, and I remember when I was a little girl and my father used to give me piggyback rides. Then I could also have a kind of tingling inside. One evening I wanted to continue tingling. When Lovis tucked me into bed I pressed my legs together and kept thinking about piggyback riding on my father's back. That tingling feeling came back, and so did my mother. As she was approaching my bed, she smiled and told me that such things would become cosier when I grew up and fell in love with a boy. I didn't catch the meaning of what she said at all. I was more like scared that she was angry with me. Perhaps she wasn't.

The tingling I had in those days was a child's tingling. The thing I'm feeling today is something else. When I was a child, the tingling existed only at a little spot in my body. Actually, it was somewhere between my legs, kind of. But the tingling I'm feeling now is a feeling that I have everywhere. It starts from my toes and rushes up to my head. Or maybe it's the other way around.

He and I have met several times since we had that jumping contest across Hell's Gap. The first time, I was just walking about in the forest and I suddenly caught a glimpse of him. The tingling came back and I didn't dare approach him. I tried to hide behind the trees by the brook instead. Me, Ronia, a girl who used to be so cocky and proud! But he spotted me and came over to me and we talked for a while. Suddenly I just wanted to remain there forever and the tingling feeling moved up to my breast. I felt like I almost couldn't breathe. At the same time, I wanted to return to Matt's Fort as quickly as possible. It's like that with me a lot these days. One minute I want to do something, and the next minute I want to do something completely different. Sometimes I even want to do two different things at the same time. It's just as if there's a gap inside myself these days!

What's happening to me? I don't recognize myself. I have other strange feelings, not only the tingling one that I've been describing. I also feel quite lonely sometimes. The other day, it happened again. I sat there right in the middle of dinner. My father, Matt, was sitting at the head of the table. Suddenly, it was as if I were looking at him in a new way. I have always thought my father knows everything. But now, I felt differently as he started talking about his lifelong enemy, Borka. He said he knew all about the stupid mistakes of Borka, "the lousiest robber ever to be seen in the woods". Everyone at our table was laughing when Matt was joking and bragging. But I just felt he was being rude. On top of that I wondered to myself, "How do you know all about the things you're bragging about? Do you think everyone will believe you just because you are the chieftain of the robber band?" I guess my father had a hunch about these thoughts inside of me, because he looked sternly at me. He had that wrinkle on his forehead which always tells me that he is about to become angry. So, I didn't speak out loud but I thought I would speak with *him* about it the next time we meet. Or, maybe one day I'll dare tell Father what I think about his bragging and his manners.

While I was thinking about all this, my mother, Lovis, was ladling out the soup. "Poor little Mum," I thought. "Always doing the same work in our big household, always taking care of everyone and listening to everyone. But how often do you speak up about what you're thinking?" Once, she was whispering to me that she'd like to join the robber band on their expeditions. She had an idea of cooking some potion which they'd pour into their enemies' wineskins. The potion would make people fall asleep, and then they could just rob their belongings without using violence. "You see, I don't like all this fighting and killing," she told me. But did she dare tell Matt about her ideas? No, no, nothing of the kind! I felt she was yellow, to be honest. And I was having these thoughts about my mother, whom I always admired so much! I was on the verge of crying, but I pulled myself together and said nothing.

During the dinner, the robbers were as boisterous and merry as usual. Normally I laugh and shout along with them. But I turned completely silent. I felt excluded and a little sad. When old Noddle-Pete asked me what the matter was, I just snapped at him.

I felt bad about treating old Noddle-Pete that way. I like him so much, and he has always been like a grandfather to me. But I couldn't help getting annoyed with him. I can't explain all these new things happening inside of me. I don't understand them myself! Maybe I'll tell him about it, I mean Birk. That's his name. Once he told me that the people at Borka's Keep, that's the place where he lives, don't understand his thoughts either. Maybe he feels something similar to me. And if that's the case, then I could talk with him about how it is to feel lonely. And then perhaps I wouldn't feel so lonely anymore.

Chapter 12

No connection

Hi Eleanor!

Help! I'm stuck out here, surrounded by trees and bushes and vegetable gardens. Nothing to do. No Internet connection. Sending an SMS works about every fourth time, if I'm lucky. I'm supposed to stay here the whole week. Mum and her guy, Craig, think it's soooo nice to have me with them at their little countryside cabin. They have been longing sooo much for my company and for a chance to pamper me for one whole week. Can you believe it – one whole week? But Jesus, I don't have anyone to talk to. Well, unless you count the cows in the meadows and the cats at the farmer's. There's absolutely nothing to do. I said that to Mum and she suggested writing a letter to you.

Me, write a *letter*? I mean, that's not my style. You know how I am! Writing means writing to my friends on Facebook. That suits me fine. But right now nothing works. No connection! What am I supposed to do? I get desperate. You know I usually chat with you and my other friends several times every day, and you always help me check out what everyone else is doing. Now I'm completely left out. No pics on what everyone was doing on Saturday night. No photos, no comments, nothing. Everything is dead, meaningless, empty! Yesterday, Mum and Craig and I were sitting in the living room and I was so bored I tapped my fingers on the table all evening just to keep awake. Mum told me to stop and then she wondered, "What's the matter, my little darling?" What's the matter? The end of the world! Finito with life, that's the matter! I get so impatient that I just can't sit still. I'm used to writing on the computer, to hearing that soft clicking sound under my fingers on the keyboard, to looking at all the pics of people I know. But now what do I see? Just an empty screen, blinking "no network". I'm going crazy.

I remember when I was a little girl and received letters from my grandmother. She wrote in capitals because I was not so good at reading in those days. Sometimes she would send me small bookmarks and stickers, mostly angels and cute stuff like that, stuff I find ridiculous today.

But I liked those angels at the time, with their rosy cheeks and chubby arms. In those days, Grandmother didn't have a computer. Well, okay, she had a computer at work but she used it only for writing invoices. When she wanted to get in touch with me, she phoned me or wrote me a letter. I loved those letters. To this day I keep them in a box at home under my bed. I especially remember a pink envelope with flowers on it. I had never seen such a wonderful thing before. Otherwise her envelopes were the usual white or brown. I didn't see Grandmother that often. It was mostly during my Christmas or summer holidays. Our cabin today was actually Grandma's place in those days. When I think of it, most of the times I was together with her it was at this place. My dear grandmother, I haven't thought of her in a long time, and now when I think about her, I really miss her. What funny thoughts enter my mind when I'm sitting here with nothing to do, don't you agree?

The stationery that I'm writing on, I just found it up in the attic. The junk room, as Grandmother used to call it. That's the place where she kept all kinds of stuff, like old clothes, badminton rackets and my grandfather's pipes. "We shouldn't keep these pipes – they killed him," as she always put it. Grandfather died of cancer before I was born. I think it was lung cancer. No, now I'm getting strange again. Back to reality!

Reality – that means being connected on the Internet. My whole life is there. That's where I talk to you and all my other friends. Well, perhaps talk is not the correct word. But I show all of you what I'm up to. That's why I write on the Internet and upload my pics. I remember the first time I was about to go out on the Internet. I thought I was supposed to look out into space because that was the word they used, cyberspace. I know you're thinking that the first time I heard about Internet I was a very little girl and you're right! At other times I thought it had something to do with going fishing. I remember thinking that if my grandfather had been alive, he and I would have gone fishing with that Internet. But then cancer took him away. That's something I prefer not to think of. Weird, but writing this letter just seems to make me fall into such death thoughts all the time. Facebook is much better! No one who is writing on Facebook is dead! By the way, I wonder if they keep your Facebook profile when you're dead. Does it matter? I don't know, but I can't stop thinking about it.

Facebook, yes . . . I wonder how my grandmother could cope with life when she didn't have all the stuff we have today. When she was little they didn't even have a TV set! She used to listen to the radio. She told me that when she was a child, she thought the voices from the radio came from people sitting inside the receiver. Once she worried that they didn't have food in there. So she put her sandwich on top of the radio set so the people inside wouldn't starve to death. Poor dear Grandmother! Can you imagine doing such a thing? It would be like if I put a hamburger on my hard disk, right?

While I'm sitting here writing to you, I'm getting a lot of thoughts that I usually don't have. You won't believe it but I'm getting a little sad. Strange, me who is so upbeat and on the go all the time. I always have a lot of ideas about doing stuff and having fun, but now I'm just sitting here. I'm thinking kind of inwards. I'm thinking of my grandmother and about things that happened when I was a little girl. I remember being afraid. I didn't dare to go up to the attic. I thought there was a man living up there who was going to grab me. I didn't have any clear idea of why he would grab me or of what would happen after that. I just knew I was afraid. To tell you the truth, I'm still afraid. I don't like going up to the attic when it's dark. Well, I know it's not dangerous, but that's the way it is. After all, how can you know for sure about stuff like that? I can't help getting the creeps up there with all those old boxes and sacks. What's worse, the light doesn't always work. Once it went off right when I was in the middle of the staircase. I got dead scared, dashed down and stumbled on the last step and just slid down into the living room. Mum rushed to me from the sofa and said she would put a plaster on my knee. I made a total fool of myself.

Wow! This is becoming a letter to myself – almost like a diary. Here comes Mum with a stamp. Should I or should I not? Okay, I might as well send these pages to you, Eleanor. After all, I have to admit that now and then my mother does have good ideas. I don't actually have anything special to tell you, but you can read what I've written if you want to and answer me. Whatever you do, promise me not to tell Theo about this letter. I would die if he were to read it!!

Hugs,

Maya

Response from Eleanor

My poor dear Maya,

My God! What's happened to you!? You're out there at your countryside cabin with no connection! Thank goodness you explained. I guess I sent you at least fifty SMSes without getting any answers. Poor you, now you don't know about what happened yesterday and what Linus told me afterwards. But how am I ever going to have time to bring you up to date?

I got your letter this morning. Mother came into my room and told me there was a letter for me from Maya. I almost fell out of bed. A letter! In the letter box, where you usually find the morning newspaper and some bills that annoy my father! I thought you had gone crazy. When I read it I understood that you really were in big trouble. At first, I thought you might have gone out on Twitter. Then I realized that it doesn't work either if you don't have any Internet connection. I told Dad, who said, "Why don't you and Maya use the mouth-to-mouth method?" Sometimes he says such stupid things! Oh, Lord! Well, we'll have to take everything from the beginning when I see you again. When do you get back home?

Do you know what I did when I read your letter? I checked my old diary! You know, that kind of diary where you've got a little lock, a key and stuff like that. I mislaid the key a long time ago and my brother destroyed the lock anyway. I've always kept my diary under my bed and it's still there. I just had to bend down and swoosh my hand around a little and I found it straightaway. Then I lay down and read all morning. I don't know if I dare write about these things to you. Promise me to burn this letter when you have read it! I mean it! In old novels they always do such things, preferably in open fireplaces. Then they sigh and stare dreamily out the window. Maybe you don't have any fireplace in your cabin, but you have got windows, haven't you?

When I was a little girl I wrote about all sorts of things in that diary: what we had for dinner, whom I was in love with and the teachers we had. Do you remember "the String", our PE teacher? I was secretly in love with him. I had forgotten about that but I found it written in my diary. He was sensationally old, at least twenty-five, and then he had these hopeless glasses, you know, those ridiculous small round ones. But when he showed us how to get onto the trapeze, we saw his muscles. They were amazing! And we just couldn't help looking between his legs – you know, all the girls in the class couldn't stop giggling. I guess we were all in love with him. Remember how he used to play in a handball team? We went to see his matches. Nowadays, I think handball is the most boring sport ever. I wrote about many other things I kept thinking about some years ago. Now that I've read my diary, some new thoughts have come to me. You know, the kind of thoughts I would never write on Facebook. I would rather die! They were scary thoughts but exciting at the same time.

It's time to hurry to the post office to send my letter to you. Oh, hell, I've got no stamps! Posting letters is such a pain! With e-mail, you just have to push a button, easy peasy! Now I must go to the store and buy a stamp before closing time! But wait a minute, there's quite a good-looking guy who just started working there, so it's not so bad . . . But make sure you're back for the weekend and don't forget Ali's birthday party. Everyone will be there.

Much love from Eleanor

Reply from Maya – the real thing

Hi Eleanor!

Thanks so much for answering my letter! You mentioned that reading your diary gave you scary thoughts. By the way, what did you mean by scary thoughts? What thoughts did you have? You know, I'm wondering because I have started having really spooky thoughts myself. Lately I have, for example . . . No, I'll have to tell you later when I get home. Well, okay, I can't wait. I'm going to tell you now. Do you remember when we were in Uppsala this spring, just after I turned fifteen? It was on a Saturday evening and we were checking things out, looking for some fun. I took a lot of pics and uploaded most of them except for some secret pics of a guy that I thought was super-good-looking! I saved those pics in a separate folder. That was a cool idea, because now I can look at them even if I'm not connected to the Internet! Once I start looking at them I just can't stop. Blah, this is getting too embarrassing! I don't even know who the guy is! I guess there are thousands of guys in Uppsala, so I'll never find him. But I can't stop thinking that one day I'll skip class and take the train over there, get off at the station, and he'll be standing there, waiting for me. Then again, I realize how stupid I am. I'll never see him again! But that does not stop me from getting a warm feeling inside when I look at these pics. You know that kind of feeling you get when the guys put their hands on your breasts. Oh, Lord, I sound as if I was fourteen years old. But if you were to see him, he's so gorgeous that you would get completely . . . Well, then thoughts come into my head where I see him and me together. You just can't write about things like that on Facebook.

Yesterday as I was browsing through the pics, my mum entered my room. I shut down the screen at once and turned around. "What do you want? You really should knock on my door before just entering like that," I said. "Well, young lady, I did knock but you didn't answer so I thought you were somewhere else," she snapped at me. Whoops, that was embarrassing, because it meant that I had been so deep down in my thoughts when looking at the pics that I didn't even hear her knocking! Mum must have guessed something because she said, and now she sounded friendlier, "One day, the things that you're in the midst of right now will turn into some nice and warm memories." She stroked my hair, but I shook her hand off my head. I mean, she was trying to be nice, but I felt there was one thing she didn't understand: these thoughts welling up inside me when I looked at the pics of the Uppsala guy, they were not nice and warm! Well, okay, actually they were, but they were something else, too. They were scary!

How can these thoughts be nice, warm and scary, all at the same time? There's something about that nice and warm thing that frightens me. I can't control it – maybe that's why! I tell myself, "Maya, get a grip, you don't know the guy, you'll never find him, forget him!" But then I can't. I just have to get out of bed, turn on the computer and open that folder again. That's what makes the whole thing scary! You can turn on a computer or a cell phone – and you can turn them off. But these thoughts about the Uppsala guy, no way! Before I had them, I looked at my life as being entirely out there, like everything about me could be seen on the Internet. What was on Internet was the real thing and the only thing. There I could see the people I meet, what you and the other guys did last weekend, what you all like and what you don't like. Everything, you know. But what about these thoughts of mine? What's going on with them? It's as if I'm standing in-between. Here I am where I can check inwards and outwards. I didn't think that way before. All these thoughts and feelings inside, I had not listened to them before. And now that I listen to them, I just can't turn them off! I mean the thoughts about Grandmother's attic, Grandfather's cancer and that Uppsala guy I took some pics of but never dared to approach.

I guess you think I've turned completely crazy out here in the wilds. Promise me that you don't believe I've become too childish! Yes, I'll go back home just before the weekend. Jesus, how cool, Ali's party, I will wear my new jeans, you haven't seen them yet. They fit me so perfectly. I feel like they were made for me!

Lots of love from Maya

Response from Eleanor

My poorest, my dearest Maya,

I really think you should come home as quick as a fly. It's not that I think *you* are crazy, if that's what you suspect. It's rather that I think *both of us* are going mad! When I first read your story about the Uppsala guy, I, well, I have to admit it, thought you were rather childish. I mean, getting a crush on a guy you don't know and will never meet again! "Doesn't she have more important things to do?" I asked myself. I was almost going to call Clara and tell her about it and try to figure out if we could do something for you. But then I thought that wouldn't be fair to you. After all, we're best friends.

Then Ali called and asked something about a CD which he wanted me to bring to his party. We were talking for an hour or so about that CD, even though I told him from the start that I didn't have it! Afterwards, I felt wonderful. Suddenly I thought, "Maybe this is what Maya means when she's speaking of her nice and warm feelings. There's nothing scary about that!" To be honest, for a while I felt more mature than you and I felt we had to talk about this when you make your way out of the jungle and return to civilisation.

Then something weird happened. After my telephone call with Ali, I went back to my room. I thought of our letters, the thing about the diaries, your grandpa's pipe in the attic, and whatnot. "What about our attic?" I wondered to myself. Up I went, and started poking in my boxes there. One was labelled "Eleanor's Toys". I looked at it, and after some hesitation I opened it. Guess what I found: my set of Barbie dolls! Luckily, I had my green jacket on, the one with the big pockets, so I tucked some toys and dresses into them and sneaked down to our apartment.

Of course, my father saw me entering and asked, in his usual teasing voice, "Found anything special in the attic?", but I didn't answer him. I just went back to my room and waited for him to leave home and go to his office. You know what I did then? I will tell you, but not until you've promised not to tell *anyone* about it. You hear me? There's a death penalty for breaking that promise! Okay, here I go: I started playing with my Barbie dolls. The thing was about Barbie having met a guy in New York. They had just cast a glance at each other, when Barbie had been shopping on 5th Avenue. But she couldn't forget about him. Then I had Ken trying to comfort her, but it didn't work out well. Barbie just had that NY guy on her mind and couldn't pull herself together. She stopped eating, Ken was desperate and her parents said she'd become anorexic. They started talking about sending her to a clinic. At that moment, I heard my brother entering the kitchen, so, quick as lightning I hid the dolls under my bed.

When my brother had left the kitchen, I didn't dare take up this game again. I had become scared, you know! Was I afraid that my brother would find out about the dolls? Yes, I was, but that wasn't all. The thought hit me that my game was a bit similar to your Uppsala guy thing. "Love never to be fulfilled" – that really sounds like the title of an old novel, doesn't it? Then I thought about Barbie having become anorexic. I mean, I had imagined that thing to have happened. I recalled last year when I had a crush on Pete, who said I left him completely cold. There was a time when I couldn't eat, sleep, be awake or do anything! Then there was all the fuss with my parents worrying about me. Well, I worried myself, to tell you the truth. I never want that to happen again! After thinking about my Pete story, I thought, "What if Maya becomes anorexic in front of her PC? What if she stops eating, just dreaming along, and ends up in a hospital?" So please, Maya, come home soon! You're my best friend and I don't want you to starve to death in the woods. Come back and let's party at Ali's place next Saturday!

Your best friend,

Eleanor

Chapter 13

The first time that I saw you

The first time that I saw you,
It was a summer's day.
The morning sun was high in heaven's blue.
And all the meadow's flowers,
In colours fresh and gay
Stood round and bowed politely two by two.
So soft the wind was whispering
And down upon the strand
The rippling wave crept fondly
Toward seashells along the sand.
. . .

'Twas like a song from Paradise,
And there above us winging
Far, far away and hard to see,
The little lark was singing.

From "The Songs of Frida" (Birger Sjöberg, 1922, translated by Helen Asbury, in: Allwood, 1983)

Our letter box is empty. It is time to sum up what we have learnt. We begin this chapter with a romantic song about falling in love. It was a summer's day, and Mother Nature was looking benevolently at the lovers. Though unknown to most English readers, the song is well known to nearly every Swede, at least from our generation. What has it got to do with our psychoanalytic dialogues with children and youngsters? How does it relate to the Land of O – that is, the inflammable and incomprehensible, often also anguished and sad inner world of our young patients? Our answer is as follows: when we meet a child we get an instant image of the initial moments of the "first time that I saw you". This internal photograph is engraved in our memory, ready to be retrieved during the weeks, months and sometimes even years of work with the child. As that work is slowly progressing, the image will expand into a complex map of the child's Land of O. More exactly, it is a map that we draw together with the child.

Our "psychoanalytic instrument" (Balter, Lothane & Spencer, 1980) is activated from the very first seconds of our first encounter and then continues to operate throughout our contact with the child. It helps us register what we see and hear from the child and also what we feel inside of us. Anyone who asks us, "Could you please explain this child's behaviour?" is probably hoping for an answer such as, "Well, it is because of this or that factor in the child's background or because of this specific circumstance operating right now." But we are seldom able to answer in such a manner. In contrast, our instrument may inform us that "I noticed a kind of affected and spurious atmosphere between me and Linda, and I do not understand why." We related that experience in Chapter 10, "Letter from the volcano". Another example occurred when the analyst was thinking to himself, "Here is baby Frida in front of me and she is screaming at the top of her lungs. I wonder if she had a bad time with her mother this morning and I also wonder why" (Chapter 7, "We don't look into each other's eyes"). Or perhaps, "Emma seems dead scared of me today. Could it have anything to do with the fact that I am using a new perfume with a strange scent?" (Chapter 6, "You'll be deader than dead").

Our psychoanalytic instrument collects signals from things we see and hear, and smell and feel and, last but not least, from our own thoughts and feelings. After having received and reflected on these impressions we are able, little by little, to relate our reflections via comments to the child. The psychoanalytic process thus gets started and proceeds. Here is a remarkable and recurrent experience: as we browse – backwards in time, as it were – through our notes from our very first meetings we are able to see how the child, unconsciously to herself as well as to us, was already conveying several essential aspects of her problems during our first meeting. Importantly, however, it is only in retrospect that we are able to collect these impressions from our first meetings, have a look at them in the light of the ensuing therapy sessions and conclude, "Aha, this was what you wanted to tell me – the first time that I saw you!" We are now going to share two of our first meetings in order to explain what we mean.

The song quoted in the chapter's beginning describes how the first meeting with another human being may affect us strongly. All our senses are working in unison to take on board as many impressions as possible: not only of the beloved but also of the surroundings. If this describes the experience of love at first sight, what has it got to do with an analyst's first meeting with a child? We believe the similarity resides in the state of mind; both the lover and the analyst have alerted their ability to receive impressions. This makes them prone to become strongly affected on an emotional wavelength. To be sure, their expectations are very different; the lover wants to get to know the beloved and win her, whereas the analyst also strives to establish rapport with the child but with the aim of helping her. But common to both are their intention to build a relationship, their emotional commitment and their openness to receive new and unexpected impressions. Nota bene: this openness is directed not only towards the beloved or towards the future child patient. The lover and the analyst also direct their openness inwardly towards themselves but in ways that are not identical. Whereas the lover is immersed in a feeling of heightened self-awareness, the analyst is trying to understand his or her emotional reactions vis-à-vis the child. To illustrate these processes, we would now like to relate the very first meeting that Majlis had with a young girl named Fatima. Just like the meeting in the poem, it was memorable and full of impressions – but it was hardly as romantic.

The first time that I saw you, Fatima

Fatima is a five-year-old girl whose parents were referred to me, Majlis, to get help for their child. They told me that she is very shy and does not dare speak out concerning her opinions, either at home or at preschool. The family is Muslim and the parents are asking themselves if she perhaps is being harassed by the other children "because she is different from the other kids." When their preschool lunch has pork in it, Fatima is served vegetarian food. She seems embarrassed about wanting special food there and the parents add, "When we ask her if that's the problem, she gets annoyed with us. 'Leave me alone', she says." When the family is out in public, her mother wears a shawl. The parents add, "That's another thing that seems to trouble her, but we just can't get her to talk with us about it!" They have heard that children can be depressed, so they are wondering, "Is Fatima depressed?" At home, she is exaggeratedly nice to her younger brother even when he is doing things to provoke her, "like all children do", the parents hasten to add. Her behaviour seems forced and artificial. They ask themselves and me if Fatima might be more annoyed with her brother than she dares acknowledge.

When Fatima entered my office the first time, together with her mother, she looked around in a shy and more or less frightened manner. She obviously did not want to be alone with me. She indicated to her mother that she should sit next to her on another chair but when her mother did so, Fatima got up immediately and sat in her lap instead. On the table in front of her, Fatima saw a sketch block and some crayons. I asked her if she liked to draw. "Mmm," she replied with an anxious glance at her mother. Then she picked up a crayon and drew a house. It took a long time to draw it because she did so with great care. When she had finished, she allowed me to have a look at it. At first it gave me a rigid and conventional impression. But in one corner I caught a glimpse of a tiny character. "That's the dog," Fatima told me when I asked her. "It's got teeth," she added. That part of the drawing gave a more lively impression.

Fatima noticed that I had little finger puppets made of felt cloth on my table. They represented different animals. "My rat," she said as she found a rat and put it on her finger. The rat started chasing an elephant, who was grunting loudly and angrily. I confirmed to Fatima that the elephant was grunting and she commented, "The elephant is evil." "So that's why the rat was chasing the elephant," I said and she nodded. The same thing happened with the crocodile, which also deserved to be hunted by the rat. The character of the game was slowly changing. With the animals still on her fingers, she now let them chase each other on her mother's body. The rat was hiding inside her mother's cardigan while she pressed the elephant under her mother's shawl and up towards her ear. Her mother started looking a bit embarrassed but said nothing.

Fatima tore a sheet of paper off of the sketch block. She drew a sheep, wadded it up and pushed it against her mother's eye. She anxiously sought to give an impression that it was just a "funny game", as she called it. However, her mother did not look so playfully at what was going on. "It's a boulder," said Fatima and indicated the wadded-up paper ball she had made. "A bomb," she added later. She let it approach the rat, which at that point was near Mum's neckline. She still wanted to give the impression that she was just playing. All of a sudden she started to call the paper ball "a ghost" while at the same time she was becoming visibly agitated. Just as suddenly she said, "This didn't actually happen here. It all happened on Iceland. No, I guess it was in Africa." Towards the end of the hour she put all the animals on top of the drawing of that nice little house she had made. She looked at the rat, which she said lived in the house. "Now the evil elephant and the crocodile can't get the rat. From now on they must live in the basement," she assured me.

Fatima ended her first session by making "a snowman". It consisted of two balls of clay that she put together. After a while, she separated them so that she had a headless snowman that she made run about in a zigzag manner. It looked bizarre, even a bit chilling. When I asked Fatima what was happening, she did not want to talk about it. As our first meeting was coming to a close, I told Fatima it was time to stop and added, "I would like to see you again. Would you like to see me again, too?" She nodded and said, "Mmm." Her indecisive answer seemed to express some confidence in me but also some worry over what might happen at our next meeting. We agreed upon a meeting two days later.

Reflections in retrospect

My experience of "the first time that I saw you, Fatima" was touching and bewildering. I noticed that she was trying to express many emotions that were coming to the fore but that she did not seem to understand herself. Furthermore, she showed them in a way that frightened her and made her mother uncomfortable. It was admittedly unpleasant for me as well to see the rat penetrating her mother's ear and to watch the headless snowman zigzagging about in my office. I asked myself why Fatima suddenly changed the scene from my office to remote places like Iceland and Africa. It seemed to occur when she got worried about the way she was playing across her mother's body. It looked as if she did not want to acknowledge any feelings attached to her games. Bombs were falling everywhere and an elephant was penetrating her mother's ear, but everything occurred in a nice and polite manner.

Analysts and therapists have long debated how we ought to act during our first meeting with a child. To simplify matters, there are two perspectives. One of them recommends that we should be cautious and patiently wait for the child to continue her communications with us. The other recommends that we should be direct and frank from the start about what we believe the child is trying to express. The cautious analyst waits until he or she has established a confident cooperation with the child. He or she also waits until he or she is certain that the contact is functioning and that the child understands what is at stake. The cautious analyst would thus have to wait until the treatment had been going on for a considerable period of time before being able to say something like, "I think that when you're playing, it is not only that you want the rat to go after the evil elephant. I think you also want to go after your mother. When you allow the animals to poke about on your mother's body, it seems you are angry with her. Could we find out why?"

The proponents of a more direct and confronting stance maintain that therapists risk losing contact with children if they avoid interpreting the latter's anxiety and suspiciousness. If therapists wait too long, children might be frightened by the fact that their impulses are allowed to run amok. The result may be that the child wishes to interrupt the joint work. These therapists claim that children who suffer from emotional problems do not solely want to meet a nice and comforting grown-up. They are also perspicacious enough to want the therapist to be frank and honest.

Our position is to regard the child in a calm and reflective manner. We indicate to her that we are with her, that we are interested and attentive.

We try to avoid harbouring preconceived notions stemming from parents' or teachers' reports on the child. Instead we wonder about what might lie beneath what we see and hear. For instance, we might say to Fatima, "Well, Fatima, I see what you're showing me . . . aha, the rat is chasing the evil elephant. What's going to happen? This rat is really giving the elephant a hard time . . . I wonder what the elephant thinks about being treated that way by the rat?"

Donald Meltzer was a British analyst of US origin, whom we will get to know better in the commentary chapter (Chapter 15). He emphasized the importance of the analyst describing to the child what he was observing. His point was to make the child attentive and reflective about her actions. Such a position has got nothing to do with naivety or passivity. To say, "Well, Fatima, I see what you're showing me . . ." rather implies being together with the child without judgements or hasty and premature interpretations. As a result, we notice that curiosity and insights start growing in the child. Meanwhile, the analyst's registering and reflecting go on. It is as if we are putting together a mental jigsaw puzzle out of our observations and our reflections on what might lie beneath.

In the commentary on Chapter 4, "Raging with love", we will relate how the two most prominent pioneers of child psychoanalysis, Anna Freud and Melanie Klein, thought about these matters. Our "Well, Fatima . . ." philosophy stems to a large extent from our meetings and studies with Donald Meltzer. His position represents a third view in child analysis. He was aware of the wisdom in being careful with the child – but also of the necessity of sometimes being confronting. The point is to be clear-sighted, perspicacious and friendly without a grain of sentimentality. After all, there is hardly any reason for professing a naive view of Fatima's game as though it were something sweet and cute. At first she drew a nice little house. But then her game changed character and she became more and more agitated. First she sat on her mother's lap, thus using her as a kind of psychic shock absorber against the unknown psychoanalyst. After a while, Fatima seemed to change her mind. Now she used mother as a target for the attacks, as when holding the elephant on her finger and penetrating her mother's ear. Similarly, she made the boulder and the bomb. In the end she herself seemed to intuit that the attacks by the animals had something to do with her mother. Her intuition was also nourished by the fact that Mum started to squirm about embarrassedly on her chair.

Boulder – bomb – ghost. The paper ball made by Fatima changed name as the game progressed. The bomb seemed to be a weapon of attack, while the ghost seemed to be a creature who, so to speak, realized that her ferocious emotions were directed towards her mother.

In Fatima's mind, such feelings were forbidden. It was as if the ghost were waving his finger, whispering to her, "I know what you are up to, Fatima!" Then the child changed her strategy in order to keep her anxiety at arm's length. She claimed that what she was doing was not happening in the office but in Iceland, well, even far away in Africa! Next she tried to calm herself down by letting the rat inhabit a nice house. That way, she believed she could protect it. But she still could not get rid of the uncertainty that made her anxious; could the rat really feel safe when it knew that there were evil elephants and crocodiles living in the basement?

As we approached the end of our first meeting, we were at the polar opposite of the romantic aspect of the poem at the beginning of this chapter. Fatima's anxiety seemed to have taken free rein. The fragments of feelings and thoughts that she was harbouring at that point did not seem to reach firm ground at all. They were rather bouncing back at her in the shape of a bizarre snowman. He was obviously a scary character. It was easy to understand that Fatima was relieved when she heard me say that the session was about to end. But why did Fatima want to come back to me? Was it because she thought that her mother wanted her to do it? I do not think so. Fatima knew that she did not feel well and that something was wrong. She discovered that there was a lady who understood that she was not simply a cute and nice girl – but who did not condemn or censure her. On the contrary, this lady seemed to be committed to meeting rats, bombs, ghosts and all those creepy things that might reside in a little five-year-old girl. If we equate love with commitment, fidelity and a deep interest in another human being, then it was love that I experienced "the first time that I saw you, Fatima". And I hope I do not seem too audacious in assuming that there was a grain of love in Fatima as well, in parallel to all her fears and premonitions. We will soon share a fantasy that will indicate more about what Fatima might have felt "the first time that I saw you, Majlis".

Was I able to understand all these connections during the first session? And did I understand all the reasons behind everything that I saw? Of course not. We might say that I was functioning a bit like Fatima – that is, I intuited things. The child seemed to be struggling with her angry feelings, which she was not able to express clearly. Part of her rage seemed to relate to her mother, considering the events linked to Mum's ear, eye and neckline. I also noticed that she was interested in talking to me about herself. To be sure, she did not do it in a direct and undisguised manner. She rather did it in ways that are typical for all children – that is, through playing and drawing. What did Fatima intuit? Let us do an experiment and fantasize how Fatima might have thought about her very first meeting with me, Majlis.

The first time that I saw you, Majlis

The first time that I saw you, Majlis, it was a winter's day. I didn't know who you were. Mum and Dad had told me I was about to meet some lady and talk to her. I didn't know what I was supposed to talk about. But I understood that it was something important because they looked so serious when they put me to bed the night before. Lately they had seemed worried when they asked me about my friends at preschool. I didn't like their questions because I was a bit sad at preschool. I thought you wanted to talk about these things with me. I guessed you were some lady working at the preschool, a boss or something like that. But when we were on our way in the car, I realized that we weren't driving to my preschool but to another place. I had never been there before. It was a rather big house and on the ground floor there was a café. I hoped that we could have some cookies and lemonade afterwards.

Anyway, I remember that you looked rather nice when you opened your door. But when I looked into your glasses I could see myself like in a mirror. I didn't like them because they scared me a little. But then I looked at your hands. They reminded me of the hands of a nice old lady who lives in our building. She always says, "Hello love" when we meet. When we were sitting in your room, Mum and I, she suddenly looked at your door. I got very scared because I thought she was going to leave me alone with you. I said to myself, "Never in my life!" and started pulling her blouse. All of a sudden your glasses seemed even scarier and I couldn't see your eyes at all. I jumped from my chair to Mum's lap. That helped me to calm down. When I saw the drawing block and crayons, I thought maybe I should stay after all. I like drawing and I love it when adults tell me I'm good at it. I got kind of hurt when you kept looking at my drawing and didn't tell me that you liked it. At my preschool they always say, "What a nice drawing you have made, Fatima!" But you didn't. Instead, you seemed to be checking my drawing very carefully. Maybe that's why you have glasses.

Then I saw the felt cloth animals and I thought it could be fun to play with them. That thing about the elephant chasing the rat was something I made up on the spot. I like making up things. I thought it was so funny and clever the way I made the elephant poke around on my mother and climb up to her ear and press it. But I noticed Mum was squirming around on her chair. I think you might say she was inbarrassed. Or do you say embarrassed? I don't know now, and I didn't know then. I just knew that Mum wasn't comfortable with my rat and elephant. That sure gave me a creepy feeling, but I still wanted to go on playing with the animals and make them chase each other.

Suddenly I got the idea that my animal game wasn't going on for real in your office. It was in Iceland. I don't know why really. I've never been there. Iceland – does it mean that it's cold up there? I thought Africa might be warmer, so that's why I changed Iceland to Africa. I didn't know why I chose Africa. I've never been there, but I know it's hot in Africa and that the people are black. Of course, elephants live there as well. Yes, maybe that was the reason I said Africa instead of Iceland! The funny thing was that these places, Iceland or Africa, just popped out of my mouth and I didn't think a second about either one of them. But you seemed so curious. I liked the way you kept asking me stuff but I thought it was kind of weird too.

The first time that I saw you, Anthony

Six-year-old Anthony's arrival at Björn's office with his mother marked the beginning of a bewildering encounter. On the one hand he impressed me as a charming boy with big, open and curious eyes. On the other hand he seemed restless and frightened. It was extremely difficult to understand his way of using words. He held a blue crayon in his hand and wondered if it had the same colour as the white wall. He wandered about in my office and named every colour he could see around him. He asked me if my red and white striped cushion had the same colours as the moon. Everything seemed to be fluid. The meaning of a certain word seemed to change from second to second. I got this impression, for example, when I asked him about a drawing. "It's a sky, no, a star. A house, no, a window," he told me. This is what the drawing looked like. It gives an even more indistinct impression than when Anthony first presented it, since he started to rub out parts of it as soon as he had made it.

Anthony said something about his parents which I did not catch. Sometimes he stammered and sucked in air in a jerky way. He seemed to do so mostly when he got worried. I also noticed that his way of walking about my office was somewhat stiff and awkward.

I felt uncertain and worried. Could psychotherapy really help this boy? But as I was looking at the heaven and the stars in his drawing I also reflected, "Maybe he feels like a tiny little chap in a big and incomprehensible universe." After a while he made a ball of plasticine, which he said was a "snake". He immediately put it aside and out of sight. Was he afraid of it? Our interaction was quite hard to grasp. He smiled, but I did not know if it was because he wanted to be nice to me, or wanted to avoid me, or just wanted to tease me. He would start talking about a subject but changed it as soon as he noticed I was interested. My frustration grabbed hold of me and I asked impatiently, "You mentioned your mum and dad earlier – what about them?"

Anthony instantly jumped into action. He went over to a cupboard, opened the door on the left-hand side and took out some more crayons, paper and plasticine. Then he tried to open the door on the right-hand side. But it was locked. He grabbed the handle and looked straight at me with a stunned expression. Was he desperate or frightened? I could not be sure.

Björn: You want to get into the other half of the cupboard?
Anthony: Mmm.
Björn: But you are not allowed to.
Anthony: I want to! I've got to!
Björn: What do you think is inside the cupboard?
Anthony: A worm, no, a snake. Open the door!
Björn: I want it to stay closed.

Anthony became visibly annoyed and soon anxious as well. He left the cupboard and walked to the front door. There was a Venetian blind covering the window of the door. He grabbed it and started crying. He wanted to go back to his mummy, who was waiting outside.

Anthony: I'm afraid of the blind!
Björn: Tell me about the blind!
Anthony: It's dangerous, it bites!

The closed door

Twice Anthony stood in front of a closed door, and each time his anxiety became evident. At other times it was rather I, Björn, who felt I was standing in front of Anthony – just as if he were a closed door. I intuited that there was something interesting behind his odd behaviours, but I could only guess what was happening inside of him. During the session, Anthony opened his "door" and left it ajar and thus enabled my roaming guesses to get a foothold. At first I was so frustrated that I heard myself asking him about his mum and dad.

Obviously, my question about his parents was not very well put at such an early point in our contact. It was a bit pushy, but it also proved to be productive. It had a strong effect on him, as shown by his anxiety at the cupboard door. It would have been easy for me to open the door but I maintained the "psychoanalytic frame", a concept that we will discuss in the commentary on Chapter 3, "Why are they doing like that?" My task was not to be a nice and obliging playmate to Anthony. It was rather to help him deal with something that was causing him great pain. This "something" became a bit clearer after he grabbed the Venetian blind. At the same time, that event raised even more questions, such as, why would a Venetian blind wish to bite a boy who is longing for his mother? When Anthony walked to the blind he became afraid, but I also noticed a trace of violence. He banged at the window rather roughly. What did he want to express by doing that?

Anthony seemed to wish to enter into something from which he felt excluded. If he tried to penetrate into the locked part of the cupboard, he would be attacked by a snake or a worm. A boy who wishes to have something that he cannot get might become annoyed or frustrated. Alternatively, he might just want to leave the place. But for Anthony things were different; he was attacked. This must imply that his wishes seemed dangerous to him. Unless he divested himself of them, they would return to him concretely – for example, in the shape of a snake, a worm or a biting blind. The difference between the snake and the worm on the one hand and the biting Venetian blind on the other is parallel to the difference between Fatima's rat and elephant contra her headless snowman. After all, snakes, worms, rats and elephants exist in reality. They can be recognized and identified by name, and everyone knows that they are dangerous in one way or another. In contrast, Anthony's Venetian blind and Fatima's snowman give an unreal and bizarre impression. In our interpretation they represent ghastly, biting fragments of feelings and thoughts. This quality makes them more frightening to the child than ordinary animals would be.

As I was summing up the impressions of my first meeting with Anthony, I felt bewildered. I felt hopeless and powerless, and I seriously wondered if I would be able to help him. Of course, that question had a realistic component which every analyst must face. Obviously, psychoanalysis cannot help every child with emotional problems. But the question also needed to be understood with the help of my psychoanalytic instrument. My doubt emerged when I felt bewildered and insecure during our first meeting. If we view things from that perspective – that is, whether psychoanalysis would be of any help for this boy – we might view my feelings as a reflection of Anthony's personal anxiety and deep sense of insecurity. In other words, my doubt might have an ingredient stemming from my countertransference, a concept we will discuss in the commentaries to Chapters 3 and 10, "Why are they doing like that?" and "Letter from the volcano". Perhaps my reactions to Anthony also reflected the feelings of his parents, who had told me how insecure and bewildered they felt about their son.

What made me decide to suggest to the parents that Anthony should start psychoanalysis with me? And what made me decide it right there at our very first meeting? In what ways did I think it could contribute to improving things for him, beyond the neuropsychiatric treatment in which he was already taking part? The first two questions can be answered by the event of the cupboard. My question to him about his parents triggered his anxiety and crowded out his earlier strangely cheerful and fluid behaviour. This event, plus the fact that he kept trying to tell me how frightened he was, made me feel that I had a potential interaction partner in the child. That is why I suggested that he should start treatment with me.

How can psychoanalysis assist in a child's development? Every child or youngster has the right to have an adult willing to listen to him or her. Painful thoughts and feelings might be talked about with the teacher in the schoolyard, with the parents at bedtime or perhaps at a scheduled meeting with the school welfare officer. Psychoanalysis also offers such a possibility, though it is obviously a more demanding and qualified undertaking. Furthermore, it is not suitable for everybody. But when the parents have not been able to help their child at bedtime, or when talking with the teacher or the welfare officer at school is not enough, what are the parents supposed to do? It is our position that a psychoanalytic therapy might contribute to a decisive turning point in a child's life. We often do not know beforehand whether a boy or a girl is suited for psychoanalysis. But during my first meeting with Anthony, I concluded that psychoanalysis would stand a chance of helping him. Of course, I could not know to what extent his neuropsychiatric symptoms would improve, but I felt convinced that psychoanalysis might be an important forum for him. It would offer him a place where he could talk about how confused he felt being "a little star in a big sky".

The first time that I saw you, Björn

Let us now imagine how Anthony experienced our first meeting: "I hardly remember. There was a big room. It was very big and you were very big too. Everything was big. There were blinds. We don't have blinds at home. I'd hardly ever seen anything like that. At first I liked it. But I didn't like for Mummy to leave me, and that made me feel scared of the blinds. But I said nothing. Back then, I couldn't say so much. All the grown-ups were always asking me questions, talking and looking worried. But I couldn't say anything to them because I didn't know what to say. Another thing was that I had something inside of me, something that kept whirling around and making me scared. I didn't know what it was. My usual way of dealing with it was to run around in circles. I could do that at home in my room or in our yard. Then Mum would tell me to stop it. She didn't understand that I did not do it to be mischievous. I was just trying to get rid of that something inside of me.

"I was running about in your room, too. You didn't tell me to stop – I recall that now. Instead, you seemed curious about it. That was funny. I remember that I was afraid of you. I had never met you before, so I guess that was one reason for my being afraid of you. As for your curiosity, well, I liked it but it also scared me. I thought that if I could just get out of your place, I could be calmer. That was when I grabbed the blind. But then I thought, 'If I run away out to the street, Mum might not be there. A truck might come driving along and I just hate trucks. They scare me.' So

I pulled hard on the blind a little and then I stopped. I kept looking at you and you looked stern-nice or maybe angry-happy. Everything was so new to me. At that moment, your blind really looked scary, kind of tiger-like. Was I afraid!

"But I remained in your room. It seemed like you wanted me to stay there. If you hadn't wanted it, you could have put me out when I pulled on your blinds. Afterwards, I told Mum what I had done. She told me that it costs a lot of money to fix broken blinds. It made me feel strange that you wanted me to come back to see you. After all, I almost made you lose a lot of money! Money is important. I know because Mummy and Daddy have told me. So I pretended to myself that you had a pipeline inside your building. As soon as I got to your place, some money would run through that pipeline down into a box that you had somewhere in your office! I thought about the pipeline and the money every time I came to see you, even though I didn't tell you about it. Actually, thinking is great fun. I just wish I wouldn't get so afraid when I do it."

Chapter 14

The last time that I saw you

When we have been working for a long time with a child in psychotherapy, we tend to think back to "the first time that I saw you". The bewildering events during the first meeting, such as those involving headless snowmen and biting blinds, have been followed up in fascinating conversations. In contrast, a feeling of monotony has beset certain sessions since nothing special has happened. The therapist has experienced a lot of feelings towards the child, from tenderness and warmth to frustration and vexation. The child has continued his development, from being ensnared by incomprehensible symptoms and rigid behaviours to establishing more playful and creative ways of relating to his Land of O. In other words, the child has become more acquainted and at ease with his incomprehensible, unconscious and unfathomable internal world. To put it similarly and briefly in Swedish – if you recall our little language lesson in the first chapter – he is no longer as afraid of his *obegripliga, omedvetna och outgrundliga inre värld*.

What about our impressions from our first meetings? Were our intuitions correct? Did the map develop in the directions which initially were only hinted at – via a strange drawing or a game with a rat and an elephant? How did development proceed and how did our last meeting materialize? We obviously cannot note every hill and valley or every straight and winding path on the "map" that we draw with the child during the course of treatment. Let us therefore focus only on some points on the map at some distance from the starting point. One of these points will concern what may happen towards the end of therapy.

The last time that I saw you, Fatima

How did it come about when we decided that we were going to end your treatment? We had been meeting for a considerable period of time, a couple of years, when the thought emerged that you did not want to keep coming to see me, Majlis, "forever". You told me that you had started school and that you did not have as much time as earlier to come to see me. You reminded me that you played football and that you had started to go to a ballet class. And that terrible ghost of yours, your Ghost-Mum, did not really exist. That was something you had discovered and felt completely sure about in those final stages. But it took some time for you to arrive at that point. How did that come about?

The first time we met you wadded up a sheet of paper and made it into a ball. You called it "the ghost". At a very early stage, then, you showed me that this shy little girl had a lot of threads of thoughts and bits of emotions that kept worrying and frightening her. The paper ball materialized into something clearer and more expressive after a while. One day – we had been meeting for a year then – you arrived at my office quite harrowed. Your mother told me in the waiting room that you had woken up during the night and called for her. You explained to her that you had had a terrible dream about ghosts. I could see how shaken you were by that dream.

You were restless. You wandered about in my office without finding anything to do. You were usually a rather soft-spoken girl who liked to be busy and have things in order, but now you were just removing things at random from your box and from my bookcase. Nothing pleased you and you wanted to throw it all away. Then you looked at me and called out loud:

"Do something, Majlis! You don't do anything!"

I was stunned. This was a new Fatima. Of course, I had heard you complain before, but now you were doing it with such anger and force and you had fixed your gaze intently and sternly upon me!

I replied, "You are quite angry today. Angry with me."

You stopped for a second but then you carried on pulling things out. You threw your drawings on the table and all the cloth animals on the floor.

You cried out, "I was so scared last night and you weren't there!"

And I replied, "You're quite right, I wasn't there. I was away when you needed me the most. Now I understand why you are so angry with me and desperate. I know I usually say that I want to help you, but this time I wasn't there when it all happened! But we could try to see what was so terrible last night. What happened?"

You told me that you woke up in the middle of the night. There was just a little glimmer of light from your night light. You called for your mother and told her about your terrible dream about a ghost.

Then you told me, "Bah! No, let's talk about something else." So you changed the subject and said, "LOL. Do you know what that means, Majlis? No, I'm sure you don't. It means laugh out loud!"

It was strange to see you laughing when you were so angry and afraid. I told you this and suddenly you became serious. You sat down on the sofa and I got an idea, which I shared with you: "It might be a good idea to make a drawing of the ghost that appeared in your dream last night!"

You agreed and started to draw. You drew intensely, using more and more colours with larger and larger strokes. This was the drawing you made:

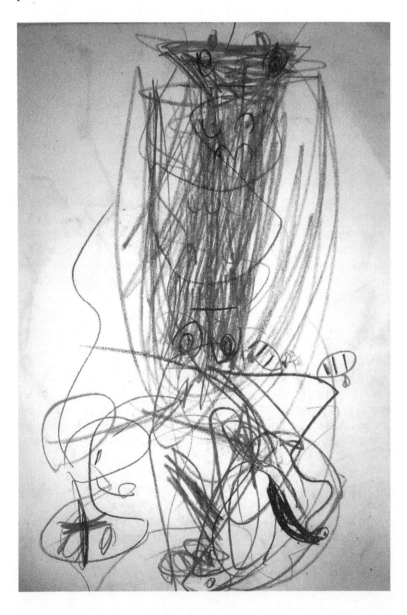

You called it "Ghost-Mum". "It was terrible," you told me. Then you got even more energetic and told me that you wanted to make another picture. You named it "An angry guy". It looked like this:

This angry guy had lots of teeth but he also had a bow in his hair. You know, one of those rosette-like things that girls sometimes think are cute to wear in their hair. I know I've seen you with one. I told you, "We know that you're afraid of the ghost in your dream. But you aren't only afraid.

You're angry as well! You were really angry with me some minutes ago. That tells us something: here is an angry guy who bites people."

It took a very long time before you were able to trust that dreams are not real but only make-believe. Nonetheless, it is important to take them seriously. It also took quite a while before you were able to understand that the biting angry guy was not out there somewhere. Actually, he was inside you! You were thinking that the biting angry guy existed only among people around you – but when I got to know how angry you might be at times, I understood that this angry guy was living inside you. But you know what? I also saw times when that angry character had been really useful to you. For example, you told me that when you were playing football you could get extremely angry. Not that you wanted to bite, exactly. After all, one doesn't bite the fellow players during a football match! But when that anger fills you up, you can give the ball a really good kick. You once revealed to me that you had scored a goal when you got that angry! And this time, it didn't scare you but rather made you superproud of yourself.

Your mother always arrived at my office together with you. She would wear her shawl and sit in my waiting room while you were with me in my office. Sometimes she would read a book with Arabic letters. They were impossible for me to understand but not for you because you already knew some of them. At the same time you were learning Swedish letters at school. From time to time, your mother brought your little brother along and read him little comics.

"Does my daughter really need to see a psychologist?" Your mother had asked me this question the first time I spoke to your parents and explained what we would be doing. "You only go to people like that if you're crazy. Our daughter is not crazy!" was your father's comment. But I managed to make them realize that you can go to see a psychologist without being crazy.

After some time, your parents began to trust me and so did you. It did not take long for you to trust me, I must say. After only a session or two, you were already able to be with me in my office, while your mother was sitting in the waiting room. Sometimes, though, you wanted to go out and check to be sure she was still there. Maybe you also wanted to find out what she and your little brother were doing while they were waiting for you. Jealousy often got the upper hand when you were talking about your brother. But other than that, you were busy doing things with me. You stayed in my room and worked with zest and commitment.

There was a time when you just wanted to play football with me. You had figured out how we could play in my little office. You were supposed to take penalty kicks while I was the goalkeeper. During these games, the shy little girl seemed to have disappeared completely and instead I saw a tough and confident football player! Everything was going smoothly and you were enjoying scoring goals against me, until one time, when I told you that I was a bit tired and had to rest for a while. You got terrified. You turned pale and sat down instantly on the sofa with your hands tucked tightly under you. It took a while but you finally told me that you were scared you had hurt me. We understood then that the strength inside you might also be terrifying to you.

There was another instance when I also realized how afraid you were of this power inside you. During one of our football games, I said you probably wanted to "beat me and win our football tournament". You got very frightened, because you thought the word "beat" meant punching or beating up somebody. You told me with embarrassment that you did not speak Swedish so well. As for me, I had another explanation. I told you that in fact the word "beat" did have the meaning you gave it but that you were having difficulties in playing around with the word's other meaning, its double meaning. It means either to punch somebody or to defeat her in a game. We knew that you liked me and that you did not want to hurt me. But sometimes, other feelings got the upper hand inside and you got angry with me. How could you be sure that your anger would not turn into beating me up? That question occupied you a great deal. Similar things happened with other people, especially your mother. You love her very much but sometimes you also got angry with her. We might perhaps put it this way: at the football club, you trained in all kinds of playing skills – how to attack, defend and become more courageous and self-assertive. At my place, you trained your mind to become more assertive and less afraid of yourself.

So you became a forward in your football team with training sessions twice a week. Then there was the ballet class as well. Once you said, "Lot of things to do!", but then you smiled and said, "And I like it!" Most importantly, you seemed at ease with yourself and you weren't so afraid anymore when angry thoughts popped up inside. I thought that you and I gave that ghost a good beating! I guess you and I realized at about the same time that it was time to say goodbye. It felt good that you were ready to move on, but, for sure, it also felt a bit sad. Taking leave of someone with whom you've been together for such a long time felt like taking leave of a friend. And that is always a bit sad, isn't it?

The last time that I saw you, Anthony

The last time I saw you, I was thinking that so many things had happened. You and I had been working together over a long span of time. You were often eager to get things done when we met. Well, perhaps, not always . . . Now and then, you were such a mischief-maker that neither of us could think properly! But when I looked back at our first meeting and at my concern about whether I could help you, I realized that things definitely had changed. You had become a keen young fellow who knew a lot of things about the world. One of your favourite subjects was geography, and by now you knew the capitals of many countries. Of course, you had started school a long time ago. You were ten years old when we stopped working together after three and a half years. A long time? Certainly, but you had a lot of work to do before you could feel more like an ordinary fellow of your own age.

At first we had to deal with the fact that you were worried almost all the time. Most of all, we observed how mischievous you were. But it soon became clear that you were not mischievous because you thought it was such great fun. The reason was rather that you were a very scared little boy. You had a lot of thoughts which we named "rowdy thoughts". Do you remember? We began to understand that your mischief in my office had something to do with all those rowdy thoughts running around inside you. As soon as you made mischief you would tell me that you had discovered some dangerous spot in my office. Once we counted up to twenty keyholes, ventilator shafts and chinks. All of them were scary and dangerous, you told me. You could not explain why, but after a while the words "rowdy thoughts" emerged. They seemed to be some kind of scary bits of thoughts. If you compare the cornflakes that you eat for breakfast with the spaghetti you have for dinner, you get a glimpse of what I mean. A string of spaghetti, well, you can always see its beginning and its end. You can follow the thread, so to speak. But you can never create order out of a heap of cornflakes, right? Such were your rowdy thoughts; they just went swirling about in your head. You wanted so badly to get rid of them. Sometimes you wanted to go to the loo in order to do so. For example, you might look with horror at the ventilator shaft and then start a quarrel or a fight with me. Suddenly, you would interrupt it and go to the loo. You returned visibly relieved, but you would not want to talk about it at all. It was as if you hoped that the rowdy thoughts had gone away with your poo.

Desperately you wondered, "What am I going to do with those rowdy thoughts? Could someone cut up my stomach and take them away?" I could really sense your agony when you asked me that question. The problem was that, of course, they kept coming back and threatening you with a catastrophe. You could not describe what this catastrophe was all about. It emerged that the rowdy thoughts included not only the thought about doing something mischievous but also the punishment for the thought. Crime and punishment all in one; things could hardly be worse!

Your work with me gradually enabled you to have rowdy thoughts without their, if I may say so, "scaring the guts out of you". In the beginning, these thoughts were some concrete inhabitants inside your body that you needed to get rid of – just like your poo. Sometimes, the rowdy thoughts appeared because you were angry with me. I remember once when I was not on time to our session. When that happened, you clearly had a lot of those "bad thoughts", as you also called them. And then there were the times when I did not grasp what you were trying to explain to me! That also made you angry with me, and whoops, the rowdy thoughts came to you right there on the spot. Now I am going to tell you about a session that I wrote down carefully. In that way, we might follow how you and I were working with your rowdy thoughts. By that time, you were eight years old.

Black Man

I think this happened on a Tuesday. Since you and I were meeting every Monday, Tuesday, Wednesday, and Thursday, this was the second day of our week. When you entered my office, you looked cocky and threw a goodbye kiss to the taxi driver. You didn't want to take your wet boots off and you snorted at me, "I can keep them on if I feel like it!" But I wanted to follow our usual procedure, so I pointed to the waiting room. You were used to taking off your boots and hanging up your coat there, so why not this time as well?

"Let's have a fishing contest," you suggested upon entering my office. You made a fishing line out of a piece of string you found in your box. You put some plasticine at one end of it, and then you cast it. You were skilled at what you were doing and seemed to be quite proud of yourself. You kept jumping up and down on the analytic couch. You told me that we were having a competition and that you kept winning all the time. My task was to admire you while you went on winning. But you seemed to ignore my comments completely. You just kept on shouting, "Hurrah, I won!" Suddenly you asked in a worried and earnest tone, "Who is afraid of Black Man?"

I was taken completely aback and answered in my "Well . . . Anthony" style, "Black Man? Well, that's a good question. It might take some thinking about."

You looked scared. You didn't want to answer when I asked you who he was or why he was scary. All of a sudden, you changed your state of mind and became the cool guy again, jumping up and down on the analytic couch. You shouted, "I am the king!" Then you added, "You are Black Man."

It struck me that I was wearing black clothes that day. I did not know what to believe about all these things. It was, to say the least, confusing! Suddenly you said, "I am Black Man."

I replied, "There is much that I don't understand. But I do notice that when you're the king, it seems that you aren't afraid of all those things that have to do with Black Man."

You nodded and went on being self-assertive and energetic. You left the office and went out into the waiting room and explained to me: "I'm going to have a TV party in this room. All my pals will be here!" I was not invited and I noted that I felt a bit sad about it. I commented that I did not get an invitation. You did not care about that at all. Instead, you kept clapping your hands and singing, "Victor and Adolf!" I didn't know anything about these fellows and, for sure, you didn't tell me.

I felt more and more excluded and wondered why these feelings emerged in me. Did I sense that there was something that you could tell me only through games about kings or songs about Victor and Adolf? You returned to the consulting room and took up your fishing game again. You cast your fishing line out from the couch while shouting, "Look, I won!"

Now I got more decisive and told you, "No, you did not win. There need to be at least two people in a game. Otherwise it is not a game and then one cannot win or lose. You are playing on your own."

You were a bit at a loss for words here. I also noted you got curious, so I continued: "I wonder about Black Man. The one you spoke about earlier. Why is he dangerous?"

Quite unexpectedly, you sat down. After a while I saw that you were looking anxiously at the flowers on the windowsill, and you told me, "Black Man eats flowers!"

Then I got an idea. I ventured, "You messed about with my flowers yesterday. I told you to stop. Perhaps you think that Black Man saw it?"

You responded promptly, "Somebody could get put in prison. The police found out about it. Be silent. We are not allowed to talk about it! Black Man eats you up. I am Black Man."

But I went on: "So you're Black Man because you made mischief yesterday and messed about with my flowers. Then somebody appeared who knows about all these things, somebody who is Black Man and who would eat you up?"

You interrupted me at once: "Shhh, be silent! Otherwise Black Man might come in here!"

I met your warning by saying, "We might try to talk about that Black Man. Maybe we'd understand why you're so afraid of him."

You replied, "No, no, no! If you talk about it, the police will know – or Black Man!"

I countered with, "I think Black Man knows about it already. You told me that you are Black Man yourself. You actually said so a moment ago."

You calmed down and I carried on: "Have you noticed that when we talk about what is frightening you, things calm down after a while and you don't need to jump about anymore?"

You replied, "I want to go to the movies . . . Do you want to come along?"

I said, "Okay!" Suddenly I didn't feel excluded any more. After all, I was invited to the cinema!

You explained, "The movie is about England. That's our name for that country. Here it is. It goes from here up to here. (You pointed at some spots on the wall.) Here is Berlin. Oops! We forgot to invite the guests. Hello, come here, everybody! Welcome!"

I wrote earlier that you are interested in geography. We must add that you were still at the beginning of your studies at the time of this conversation. The session was reaching its end. We were collecting all your toys in the play-box, and you were putting your boots and your jacket on. Then you said with a warm smile, "Bye-bye, Black King."

Not only did you seem friendly but also you had become calm and at ease. I responded, "You are more calm now. This is what happens to you if you blend the king with Black Man."

Reflections in retrospect

In the earlier phases of our work together, Anthony and I often fell back into a certain pattern of interaction. He tended either to get rowdy or to gloss over the truth, especially when he had been up to some mischief in my presence. When he did so, he always feared that I would become annoyed or punish him. But this pattern changed when he began to notice that I would rather ask him questions about what was going on. He began to regard me as well as his rowdy thoughts in a different light. During the session with Black Man, we could see that he was becoming less prone to view me as someone intent on putting him in jail. But we also noticed that his thoughts were chaotic. He really needed help to be able to think more clearly. At first he said he was Black Man and then that I was Black Man. That character evidently signified the person who does the rowdy things, the person who discovers them and the one who punishes him for it. Criminal, policeman and judge in one and the same person. It certainly would take less than that to make anyone, whether a child or an adult, scared and confused!

Another theme that we can discern in our very first encounter as well as in the Black Man session has to do with being an outsider. In the first session, I assumed he felt like an outsider when he stood in front of the locked cupboard and was not allowed to open it. He reacted by trying to escape to his mother, but stopped at the entrance door and then panicked.

To create some order in this chaos of thoughts and feelings seemed to be an insurmountable challenge to him. In the Black Man session, there is another outsider character: me! As Anthony is getting ready for his TV party, I am not invited. As a result I feel sad, like a child who has not been invited to his mate's party. I was able to process that feeling within me. I got the idea that it was actually *he* who was defending himself against some painful feeling of sadness. But as I heard him speak about the flowers, I realized that his guilt was troubling him more than any sadness. He had been messing around with the flowers, and I had told him not to do it. It is also quite possible that my comment to the effect that there must be two people in a game, and that he was playing on his own, received some energy from my feeling like an outsider. Just as in Chapter 10, "Letter from the volcano", we observe how the countertransference gets the analyst started. If we detect it and work on it, we may use it to better understand which feelings or conflicts the child is struggling with at the particular moment.

I have made a number of observations about feelings, but I would also like to emphasize that it was important to do more than talk about the emotions beneath Anthony's mischief-making. In this context I helped him to erect a framework on which he could "suspend" his thoughts. Here I gave him a kind of cognitive help or, to put it in more classical psychoanalytic terms, I assisted him in scaffolding his ego functions. I showed him how he could think more clearly when rowdy thoughts were pressing from inside and making him confused. For instance, Anthony found it difficult to understand the course of time: when we were to meet and not to meet, when it was Christmas break or summer break, when the week started and ended. All of these aspects of time were completely bewildering to him. I got the idea that we could make a calendar with one sheet for each month. The picture shows how one of them looked. Anthony drew the circles with some colours, whereas I wrote November and the figures. We could then see that the sixth, seventh, eighth and ninth of November were black for "Björn-days", the days of our appointments. In contrast, the tenth, eleventh and twelfth were yellow for weekends and days he would not see me. Thus we kept on working according to our calendar, day by day, week by week, in a rhythm that helped Anthony become more comfortable with his rowdy thoughts.

Let us return to discussing the session with Black Man. Towards the end, something important happened. The cocksure and competing royal highness yielded to a king who ruled his country in a fair way. I think that is why Anthony ended up calling me Black King and not Black Man, while smiling warmly at me. Simultaneously, he had changed his attitude and had become a fair guy who invited me to the cinema in Berlin, England. When it was time to say, "Today is the last time we meet," he definitely

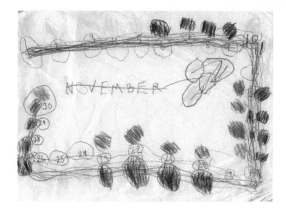

had another attitude towards me. His rowdy thoughts were still there, but they emerged as comprehensible emotions and not as enigmatic actions. When these thoughts no longer automatically led him towards rowdy actions, he became freer to think and to choose constructive actions.

Anthony became a real ace in geography and in other subjects at school. The first time we met, he made a drawing of "a sky, no, a star. A house, no, a window." Here is one of his final drawings. Undeniably, many things had evolved between the first time and the last time we met, Anthony and I.

Now Anthony drew his own universe. He put the sun (*solen*) right in the middle with the Earth (*jorden*) at some distance away. Even little Pluto could be found in the drawing. But above all, there was a place for Anthony himself. He pointed at the blue Earth and commented happily, while scribbling on the drawing, "*HÄR BOR VI*" or "THIS IS WHERE WE LIVE!"

Chapter 15

Commentaries on Chapters 2–12

Chapter 2 – The hole in the escalator

Many children are at one time or another afraid of ghosts, darkness, tigers, insects or spots on the wallpaper . . . The list is endless. Most often, such fears pass away as the child develops and acquires a new ability with which he can master his fear. For example, sometimes you see a little child who has just made a leap in his language development and has then become able to use that ability to calm himself down: "Tiger not scary, he not scary." Such fears may also vanish by themselves, though we do not understand how it all came about. It seems as if something upsetting or frightening within the child just dissolved into oblivion by itself.

Then again, some children develop fully fledged and incapacitating phobias, which need psychotherapeutic treatment. The most famous published case is the very first presentation in this genre: Freud's "Little Hans" case (1909a). Another well-known case in the history of child psychoanalysis is "Frankie" (Bornstein, 1949). As an adult man he sought analysis again, which engendered an article discussing the connections between child and adult pathology (Ritvo, 1996). There are many other instructive papers on childhood phobias (Cohen, 1989; Fraiberg, 1987; Hoffman, 2007; Renik, Spielman & Afterman, 1978; Tyson, 1978). Common to them all is that they do not regard the phobia as a mere symptom that therapy should help the child get rid of. It rather investigates if the phobia may carry some hidden meanings – for example, what the child feels and thinks about the world at large and how he experiences the relationships with his family and friends. In other words, what is the connection between the child's phobic symptom and his Land of O?

In Bonnie's case, the problem could be described as neither a transitory fear nor a fully fledged childhood phobia. It was rather a continuous, complex and painful combination of problematic behaviours and frightening emotions. Nadia, her mother, suffered from a depression after her delivery. Descriptions of postnatal depression can be found in numerous publications (Beck & Indman, 2005; Dowd Stone & Menken, 2008; Murray & Cooper, 1997; Tronick, 2007).

We need not enter into the prehistory of Nadia's depression. Suffice it to say that it constituted an important part of the psychological milieu of Bonnie's earliest months. Actually, this depression was not a preconceived notion in the therapist's mind when treatment started. Nadia was rather taciturn at first about what had happened after Bonnie's birth. Her postnatal depression and its impact on her and her daughter were rather discovered during a lengthy therapy. It started as a joint psychoanalytic treatment when Bonnie was sixteen months old. Nadia complained that her child was restless and anxious and constantly grabbing for Mum's breast when something troubled her. Intertwined with my "dialogues" with Bonnie, Nadia's story about her postnatal depression enabled us to reconstruct the baby's earliest experiences. This therapeutic work enabled a more sustained independence by the daughter from the mother in the sense that Bonnie no longer needed to grab for the breast. After some months she was weaned without much more ado. Bonnie continued alone in a traditional child psychoanalysis, during which we worked with her fears of holes and of ghosts. We understood that her restlessness and phobias seemed linked with her earliest experiences of being with a sad mother who could not contain Bonnie's anxieties. This treatment has been described in greater detail elsewhere (Salomonsson, 2014, Ch. 5).

Mother-infant interaction and depression

How is the baby affected if the mother is depressed? This question can be investigated by video-recording their interaction in a laboratory. Another method of investigation is to provide a psychoanalytic treatment for the child and the mother and in that way reconstruct past events. These two methods complement each other. Numerous research studies show unanimously how sensitively a baby reacts to being with a depressed mother. To summarize a few (Field, 2010; Goodman, 2007; Murray et al., 2010; Tronick, 2007), depressed mothers tend to be more irritated with the child, play with less commitment, be less aware of child safety issues and have thoughts of harming the child. Their babies tend to show more negative affect, and have more sleep disturbances and problems with affect regulation. Cognitive problems are more frequent among teenagers whose mothers were depressed in their infancy. To sum up, we have good reasons for committing ourselves to helping depressed mothers with infants, rather than adopting an attitude of "wait and see".

What happens between a baby and his or her depressed mother? The Harvard researcher Ed Tronick (2007) demonstrates how a mother sometimes pulls away from her child and seems uninterested in him or her.

The baby then tries to establish contact with her. Other mothers tend, in contrast, to be intrusive. By poking the baby in the tummy, or by tickling him, they seemingly want to compensate for their depression and increase their contact. The response from the baby is, unsurprisingly, to ward off the mother as well as to avoid looking at her.

Another research group under Tiffany Field (Field et al., 1988) demonstrates that these babies have developed a distinct way of communicating with their mothers. They even transmit such communicative patterns in relationships to other adults as well – for example, the staff at their preschool. Parallel to the findings in such children's behaviours, the staff members are less likely to play with and be together with them. Unknowingly, they seem to prefer being with children of non-depressed mothers. It seems that the baby has already developed a behaviour which rubs off onto the staff member. Unconsciously and despite good intentions, he or she does not feel invited to interact with the baby. This illustrates the negative interactive circles often seen among dyads of depressed mothers and their babies. Another study showing the impact on the baby was performed by the same group (Field et al., 2007). They investigated a sample of four-month-old babies of depressed and non-depressed mothers, respectively. The former group of infants showed less spontaneous interaction with their mums. All babies were then subjected to the so-called Still Face experiment, in which mothers kept their faces completely still for a short period of time. The babies of depressed mothers now showed less stress than the other children. It seems as if these babies had got used to being with mothers with low emotional reactivity. Therefore they did not find the Still-Face look of Mum as frightening as did babies whose mothers were not depressed.

Why and how does such a depressive atmosphere impact on the baby? To answer, we have to rely on psychoanalytic speculations stemming from analytic work with babies and mothers. A mother, and for that matter any one of us, can only imagine the emotional storms that might be raging inside a screaming and desperate infant, or a withdrawn and low-keyed baby. The psychoanalyst W. R. Bion (1970), whom we mentioned in our introductory chapter, emphasizes that every child – not only those who have a depressed mother – needs a particular kind of encounter with the adults in his or her surroundings. Bion's word for it is "containment", a term that will recur many times in this chapter since it is also an essential ingredient in psychotherapeutic work. In other words, it is the adult's task to receive the baby's feelings. We may think of the mother as a receiver who is working upon these feelings inside herself, in order to finally give them back to the child in a calmer and more comprehensible way. In other words, the great task of the infant's mother is to try to imagine her child's feelings. She does this by a process which Bion calls "reverie" – that is, by entering a dream-like state. In this state, she tries to understand what is troubling her baby and what he might feel or need. A succinct description of how this may come about in child analysis is provided by O'Shaughnessy (1988b).

In order for such reverie to come about, the mother needs to become, at least temporarily, a "child" once again. D. W. Winnicott (1956) named this state "the primary maternal preoccupation". For example, she needs for a moment to test how the baby might feel when being forced to wait one minute for a bottle to warm up in the microwave. If she succeeds in imagining such an emotional trial, she might convey to the child that she has understood something of this "eternal waiting". At the same time she shows the child that he had to wait simply because the milk needed time to warm up and that he was never near a catastrophe. In the end, she might say to him soothingly, "Well, well, Johnny, you surely are a hungry boy, aren't you? It is *so* difficult to wait, isn't it?"

Many psychoanalytic authors (Norman, 2001; van Buren & Alhanati, 2010; Waddell, 1998) have described how the parent-infant interaction affects the development of the child. When a mother is depressed, she often finds it difficult to contain the strong feelings expressed by her baby. Depression prevents her from "feeling into" the child's emotion. Her reverie and spontaneity when being with her baby are dampened. Such an experience seems to scare the baby. His or her terror might increase in the face of the mother's feelings of nothingness and meaninglessness. The child perhaps experiences this as being in front of a psychological "black hole" (Grotstein, 1990). We think that Bonnie experienced similar feelings when she looked down into the empty escalator. We thus do not think that the escalator reminded her of a depressed mother per se. It rather reminded her of a mother who was not able to contain all the various feelings that raged inside Bonnie. When her mother was in that condition, Bonnie's feelings could not get a foothold inside her mother.

What happens when Bonnie's feelings are not contained by her mother but rather disappear into the "black hole"? Our response is that they keep swirling around about within the child herself. The child tries to integrate them into more comprehensible experiences, but they remain splintered and incomprehensible. Bion names them "beta-elements", a term which might sound as enigmatic as the phenomenon is to the child. This abstract and even abstruse term was intended to help us understand the concrete nature of children's thinking. From Bonnie's perspective, these beta-elements appear in a highly concrete way in the form of ghosts. We remind the reader of Bonnie's terror when she exclaimed, "The ghosts eat you with the mouth they don't have." How is a little child supposed to understand such a paradox?

Nevertheless, we may look with some optimism concerning our ability to help mothers and children like Nadia and Bonnie. Our task, as Alicia Lieberman and Patricia Van Horn have formulated it (2008), is to empathize with the mother in her difficult situation – and at the same time to be frank about how we think her depression might affect the baby. This balance is not always easy to maintain. Maternal depression is almost always connected with a strong sense of guilt. The mother might easily experience the words of the therapist as accusations, and she might then feel even more worthless. In the case of Nadia and Bonnie, we managed to steer away from these reefs and were able to help them in different ways: as for Bonnie, her fear of holes and ghosts became more comprehensible to her. As for Nadia, her depression and guilt feelings decreased thanks to the process by which the analyst could contain her despair and guilt. At that stage she was able to notice that Bonnie was no longer so afraid. Even more importantly, love for her child started surging forth in the mother.

Finally, a word about the term "containment". Bion, who was an officer during WWI, intentionally used a term with a military connotation. Just as it is the task of a tank platoon to contain the enemy, the analyst must face the agonizing storms in the therapeutic encounter and remain the one who is able to think about what is going on. In contrast, the modern use of the term among psychotherapists sometimes veers towards a connotation of being empathic, friendly and understanding towards the patient. However important, this ingredient does not suffice. We also need to provide the patient with words for his "nameless dread", as Bion (1965) called it. There is thus an act of translation (Salomonsson, 2007a) involved in every act of containment. Containment also inevitably implies a relationship. There must be someone out there with whom one can talk and who is willing to listen.

Perhaps the most succinct description of containment was written two centuries ago: "All evil is mysterious and appears greater when viewed alone. It becomes all the more ordinary, the more one talks about it with others; it is easier to endure because that which we fear becomes totally known; it seems as if one has overcome some great evil" (Solomon, 2012, loc. 72). The quotation is a diary entry by a man who endured many emotional storms and suffered many desperate moments during his lifetime: Ludwig van Beethoven.

Chapter 3 – Why are they doing like that?

The Oedipus complex

According to Greek mythology, Oedipus was a king who killed his father and married his mother. After his crime was revealed, he punished himself by gouging out his eyes, and his mother committed suicide. Sigmund Freud thought that the ancient tragedy of Sophocles expressed a universal phenomenon and dilemma. The relationship of the child to his parents is a relationship of life and death. We find an excellent introduction to Freud's views on these matters in his book *The Interpretation of Dreams* (1900). In that book he uncovers, like a true Sherlock Holmes, secrets about himself. He discovers that his own dreams indicate the ambivalent feelings that he harboured towards his father, who had passed away some years prior to his writing the book. It is a fascinating mélange of a personal document and a systematic theoretical construction.

Just like Freud discovered about himself, every child seems to have divided feelings towards his parents. This is obvious in Peter's case, as well as in that of Alma (Chapter 4), who expressed such ambivalence with her succinct formulation "raging with love". These feelings certainly imply tenderness and friendship, but there is also a longing for sexual monopoly. Through this combination, many emotions enter the child's life: a sense of exclusion, anger, envy and jealousy. The child's ideas of what might constitute this monopoly depend on his developmental level. The child tends to envisage that the parents have some kind of blissful union – and he wants to share this union with one of them while excluding the other. Sometimes his longing centres around the mother, sometimes around the father. This applies to the little girl as well; she hopes to marry father, the king so to speak, while getting rid of that "queen", her mother. Or, at other times, she wishes to possess the mother while being contemptuous vis-à-vis the father.

Inevitably, such strivings must come to nothing, and the feelings in question will crash when they come up against harsh reality. After all, the parents will say no when the child expresses these wishes and the child will feel disappointed, annoyed, enraged and humiliated. What is the child supposed to do with all these feelings? Peter thinks he *must* fuss and fight at home, otherwise the "sting" within him will return. He needs help to understand that his feelings, his "finest" ones as well as the ones that are the hardest to bear, are always allowed. But, importantly, he also needs help to find other ways of expressing them than to fight.

It is obvious that Peter is struggling with his feelings about his parents' sexuality. It is also easy to notice that he is fascinated by his mother and annoyed when his father hugs her on Saturday evenings. He is also annoyed with another competitor, his little brother, but not only because the little one is stealing his mother's attention. O'Shaughnessy (1988a) has pointed out that the Oedipal threat, from the child's point of view, need not be constituted only of mother + father. He may feel threatened by a "menacing three – mother pregnant with a new baby and father" (p. 197). To Peter, his little brother is living proof of the fact that his parents do what they want in their bedroom without his permission and control. Peter also has another feeling, his envy, which makes it hard for him to realize these things and mourn them: his daddy, the king so to speak, and his mother, the queen, rule their country without waiting for permission from Peter. Our crown prince seems above all to struggle with his envy. He is envious about his parents' deciding and knowing "everything". That is why he must nag at his mother and at the analyst with the question, "Why are you doing like that?" He finds it difficult to stand the fact that there are things that we adults understand, while he does not.

The meaning and impact of the Oedipus complex are still under debate. For an interesting comparison of French and British views, we refer to a paper by Lebovici (1982). Melanie Klein (1945), who spent most of her professional life as an analyst in the United Kingdom, claimed that envy appears early in the child's life and that it is also instrumental in pushing the Oedipus complex forward. The child keeps thinking that if he could only own his parents and divest them of their power, his envy would not be so intolerable! But the child needs help to relinquish his relentless demands. How does the analyst help the child with such a difficult task? The answer is "training by the nesting-box". It takes place when you stand together with the child – outside the nesting-box – and refrain from answering all his concrete questions. In contrast, you listen to the child and try to figure out how he feels. Peter needs help with his need to control other people. He also needs to learn to tolerate that sting inside, the sting of exclusion and envy. If he succeeds, his sense of exclusion might rather function as a driving force, which will assist in developing his social capacities. He will then be able to transform his sense of exclusion into friendship and a sense of belonging. He can hopefully change his envy into curiosity for, at the end of the day, Peter is a personable and clever lad.

The psychoanalytic frame

In the commentary on Chapter 2, we emphasized containment as a central aspect of the analyst's work. We quoted Beethoven, who described the importance of sharing his "evil" with someone. We guess that he was referring to an intimate conversation with a close friend. The analyst is not a friend but rather someone who is consulted on a professional basis to assist in a child's development. In order to do something similar – but not identical – to what Beethoven was referring to, he or she needs to maintain "the psychoanalytic frame" (Bleger, 1967; Künstlicher, 1996). This term has a concrete and an abstract aspect. Concretely, it means that the analyst starts and finishes each session on time. He keeps his therapy room furnished the same way, session after session, month after month, year after year, as far as possible. If the analyst catches a cold or takes a vacation, he does not ask a colleague to substitute for him. Such interruptions are seen as natural and inevitable ingredients of therapy, and their effects are worked through during the sessions. These are general principles for psychoanalysis and psychotherapy for patients of any age.

As for the treatment of children, some special ingredients are added as well, as described in detail by, for example, Anna Freud (1926, 1965), Klein (1932), Blake (2008), Norman (1991) and Rodriguez (1999). A special issue concerns work with parents, an essential part of the treatment. The parents wish to know what takes place in therapy and if progress is being made. These wishes are understandable and must be met with great respect and the necessary information. On the other hand, it is important that the child feels, and really is, secure that he or she can reveal secrets or embarrassing matters without fearing that the analyst will reveal them to the parents. This puts a great challenge onto the analyst, who must walk the tightrope between being tactful and informative towards the parents and respectful vis-à-vis the child's right to privacy. For further reading on the complexities involved in work with parents in therapy, we refer to Badoni (2002) and Tsiantis (2000).

What is so specific about the child psychotherapeutic frame on the concrete level? Every child has a personal box or cupboard in the analyst's office, which contains material that only he or she is allowed to use. There are some toys, sheets of paper, crayons, Scotch tape, scissors and other items adapted to the age of the child. Therapists hold different opinions as to how much play material to put into the box. We think such material should help the child to express his difficulties rather than to encourage him to hide them behind a multitude of objects. From time to time, the therapist might add a new toy if the child has suggested it. Now and then, a child might bring an object from home to therapy with him. One day, Peter brought a stick from a tree to his session. "Today, we are going to make a nesting-box," he said. And so we did. Then we talked about how a little bird could sit outside the nesting-box. How might he feel? That way Peter was able to express his feeling of exclusion.

The frame is also an abstract concept. It is a way of relating to the patient and of handling one's thoughts about him. The analyst stays a bit in the background and lets the patient play the main character. In this way we give the patient a chance to make his personal "painting" of what resides inside his "nesting-box" or, to put it otherwise, to reveal details about his internal world. As for Peter, he slowly began to intuit the idea behind this frame. He was frankly angry with it at first; why did Björn not reveal whom he had been talking to on the telephone, and why all these stupid comments by him about "Well, Peter, what do you think . . . ?"

Despite his criticism Peter began to realize, by and by, the idea with the analytic frame: that it offered him the floor to tell Björn what the world was like from *his* perspective. The frame is therefore our way of being respectful to the patient. Of course, Peter saw it otherwise, especially in the beginning of our contact. He thought Björn should pay respect to him by telling him if he had a wife and children and other such personal details! In relationships other than the psychoanalytic, giving out such information would be natural and polite. But in our offices another kind of logic reigns. We want to encourage children to show us what *their* world looks like, rather than letting our own enter and colour the dialogue.

By maintaining the frame as in this example with Peter, we do not wish to be secretive or mean. It is rather that we want to confront him with an equation that he has tried to escape so far. He keeps thinking that if he were only to receive the answer to this or that question, all his worries would vanish. However, as long as he keeps sitting at the entrance to the nesting-box and nagging, his development will not proceed. His creative powers, his playfulness and his generosity will not find ways of expressing themselves. Neither Peter nor his family and friends will gain anything from such a deadlock.

Towards the end of the chapter, something important has taken place. Mum has shown Peter that she now understands that he sometimes wants to be on his own with her, which she can accept within reasonable limits. We do not know whether her understanding has come about through the fact that Peter has become a more agreeable family member, or that he has spoken explicitly with her about his wishes, or that she and her husband have had regular meetings with the analyst. We would not be surprised if it were a combination of all three factors.

As for Peter in this scene, he lets his creativity loose with an energetic drawing about eagles and little nestlings that are being threatened. Not only does he get happy about going to the zoo, but also he becomes generous and helpful to his mother and his family. Here, we notice something which Freud saw as one of the most important ways for a child to maintain a constructive attitude to the Oedipus complex: the child identifies with the parent that he has been so angry with. When Peter offers to play with his little brother, he, in fact, does something similar to what Daddy does with Mum on Saturday nights when he offers to put the children to bed so that she can relax. It is not clear how much Peter understands of the sensuality between his parents, but he has noticed the warmth and generosity between them. This is what annoys him so much – but it is also what inspires him and makes him a bit happier in the end.

Countertransference – I

Finally, some words about the concept of countertransference. We prefer to define this term as the sum total of the analyst's feelings and fantasies towards his patients, especially those feelings that are unconscious. Countertransference is a valuable, indeed an indispensable, instrument in helping the analyst to understand his patient. We will return to the concept more extensively in the commentary on Chapter 10, "Letter from the volcano". In the case of Peter, the countertransference consisted of the analyst's getting annoyed and sometimes, yes, even exasperated, when the boy kept questioning him, mocking him and occasionally throwing things at him – but also of his identifying with Little Oedipus Peter. After all, the analyst himself was a little boy once upon a time!

The countertransference also consists of something that we call a psychoanalytic love of the little seeker. Such love needs to exist if treatment is to achieve substantial results. In Chapter 13, we compared the initial meeting with a patient to the romantic poem "The first time that I saw you". There we spoke of the heightened sensitivity to impressions. We found other similarities as well; both the lover and the analyst wish to build a relationship and are deeply committed in this project. Here we want to emphasize a more long-term aspect of the "psychoanalytic love affair". Such love and commitment grow slowly during a lengthy work process where the analyst follows a human being who is struggling with painful feelings and embarrassing behaviours. This love is, of course, different from the love the analyst feels for his own children, his partner or his family, but, just as with love generally, psychoanalytic love cannot be feigned or coerced. It grows, as in the case of Peter, while the analyst watches the child trying to come to grips with himself. We think Peter noticed this, even though it was not expressed directly during sessions. It helped him stand the embarrassment when he felt like an envious and shameful little troll who kept on asking, "Why are you doing like that?"

Chapter 4 – Raging with love

How are we to understand the fact that Alma's and the analyst's encounters enable the child to deal with her worries and angry outbursts? Or, as Alma herself would have put it, "How does the angry ball inside me get smaller when I play with you?" Alma's question highlights an important tool in psychoanalytic work – that is, play. This theme deserves a digression of its own.

The meaning of play – theory

Child psychotherapy and psychoanalysis are sometimes called "play therapy". That expression might make us believe that the child, under the therapist's auspices, will relieve himself of his trouble by merely playing with the therapist. Children play for many reasons: to let their fantasy flow in unperturbed directions, to make friends, to learn about the world, to abreact powerful feelings, to have fun and so forth. The importance and the meaning of play in therapy are different than in everyday play and have been described many times in child psychoanalytic literature. Two prominent figures appear in the debate: Anna Freud and Melanie Klein. Both of them were convinced that play was a major tool in understanding and working through the child's troubles. Both of them worked with children in psychoanalysis and built theories about children's inner worlds and development based upon their playing sessions with them. But there were also clear differences between the two. Klein was of the opinion that everything that a child expresses in play corresponds directly to the adult analytic patient's free associations. As she saw it, the play was simply the child's language. Through his play, the child expresses his inner world with all its relations, emotions and contradictions. In her psychoanalytic encounters with children, Klein interpreted the various ways that the child expressed his or her conflicts and anxieties. According to her, the child expressed immediately, from the very start of the treatment, how he or she viewed the analyst as well. Therefore, she also thought that the child's play could and should be interpreted as expressing his or her transference. We will discuss this concept in our commentary on Chapter 10, "Letter from a volcano".

Anna Freud's (1926; Sandler, Kennedy & Tyson, 1990) view of the child's play differed from that of Melanie Klein's. To her, playing was not at all equal to a verbal association of an adult patient. It was rather a method used by the child to evade reality. The play was ruled by the child's wish to escape unpleasant feelings and thoughts. The analyst had to wait until some confidence was built up between her and the child. Only then would the time be right to interpret what was going on in the child's play, beneath its conscious appearance. In order for this confidence to settle, the analyst must institute a special introductory phase in treatment, according to Anna Freud. The child must be prepared in a pedagogical way. A more confrontational approach would entail the risk of the child's wanting to break off the treatment.

Melanie Klein (1932) was of the opinion that a child's lack of trust at the beginning of psychoanalysis was due to his or her destructive fantasies. The child had been harbouring such fantasies for a long time, but now in the therapy room, they came out in the open and were directed towards the analyst. It was, of course, frightening to the child to discover that an "innocuous" stroke with a pencil, or a tiny plasticine figure, could express some "bad" wish on the child's part towards the analyst. However, and in contrast to Anna Freud, Klein thought there was a risk of losing the child in the beginning of treatment unless the anxieties were interpreted immediately. Refraining from doing this might create fears in the child, since the impulses risked swamping him or her. This might lead the child to stop cooperating in treatment. The discussion concerning these issues goes on to this very day (Holder, 2005; Winberg Salomonsson, 1997). Let us now study Alma's play and how the analyst handles and promotes the process.

Alma is playing and Majlis is thinking

Majlis's basic stance is to take Alma's play seriously, no matter how incomprehensible it might seem with all the cars, trains and strange characters Alma is inventing. Furthermore, Majlis assumes that Alma wants to express her contradictory feelings through her play. The wild journeys of Little Mimi and Strong Adolph indicate those emotional collisions that threaten to blast Alma to pieces. In the midst of this emotional chaos, she experiences herself as a helpless victim. Moreover, she has become involved in a triangle drama of Alma–Father–Yvonne (or his Fiona as Alma calls her, in obvious vexation). The Oedipal conflict increases the emotional temperature in her play, as is clearly noticeable in Adolph and Mimi's passions, which keep getting wilder and stormier. "Here comes Adolph raging with love."

We have already described the theory of the Oedipus complex in the commentary on Chapter 3 about Peter, "Why are they doing like that?" Alma is working through her personal triangular drama, over and over again, with the help of Strong Adolph and the little doll Mimi. The analyst provides space and freedom to express all these emotions, and she also guarantees that things will not get out of control. Alma's play indicates, more clearly than in our story with Peter, the sexual confusion pertaining to the Oedipal drama. Different themes run pell-mell; one is romantic, as when the enamoured suitor Adolf whispers to his darling Mimi, "My darling, my beloved woman." In another scene, Mimi behaves more like a heroine from a Wild West movie. This character seems intended to ward off Mimi's, or perhaps we should say Alma's, fears of sexuality. That is why, as Alma says, "her mother spoke to Mimi about him and she got frightened." We guess Alma's fears centred around various aspects of sexuality: how to combine it with love, what happens between a boy and a girl when they do that thing together and so forth. Will she dare "open up for you", as Mimi says to Adolf? Will Alma be able to combine love ("those hearts in the air") with sexual desire ("those bold snakes and all those things")?

Many children experience being little as troublesome and humiliating. Alma is enraged by what she sees as the injustice of adults' privileges. She refuses to be someone who does not know everything. She hates going to bed earlier than the grown-ups and not to be the one to decide which duvet to buy at IKEA. Such feelings tend to prevent many children from learning about the world. Learning something new implies, obviously, that the child has not known about it from the start. Some children try to solve this dilemma by maintaining that they do not have to learn. They know everything already! Alternatively, they maintain that it is not important to learn things, like how to count and to read and write. Alma's comment, "Oh sekoor, sillvoo play!" expresses her conflict of being little and big, all at the same time. She claims that she speaks French now, in her grandiose way of explaining that the newcomer at preschool taught her some French expressions. At the same time, we may note the import of her little expression: "Au secours, s'il vous plaît". Thereby she indirectly expresses her need of help and her hope that she may find important support in Majlis.

Finally, a comment on the caption of this section: Alma is playing and Majlis is thinking. In our commentary on Chapter 3, we discussed the analytic frame. It is the task of the analyst to create it and to introduce it to the patient. As we wrote earlier, it has many ingredients. Here we would like to add that "play therapy" is not to be understood to mean that the analyst and the child are just playing with each other. Psychotherapy is something altogether different from ordinary play situations, such as when a grandmother plays hide and seek with her grandchild. Children rarely need to be enticed into playing. It is rather that they want the adult, also the analyst, to join them. But the analyst's main task is to think about what goes on inside the child and what he or she is trying to express. The analyst needs to pull back a little and think, rather than letting herself be swallowed up enthusiastically in a joint play. After all, a child's play contains so many messages which the analyst needs to interpret. One day Alma said on a sour note to Majlis, "You're such a boring playmate. You're just *thinking* all the time!" In this context, we would take those words as a compliment from Alma: Majlis is fulfilling her task – not as a playmate but as a psychoanalyst. This treatment is discussed in more detail in a separate paper (Winberg Salomonsson, 2013).

Chapter 5 – Here comes Pippi Lundström

Pippi Longstocking is a well-known literary character created by the Swedish author Astrid Lindgren. She is loved and admired by children throughout the world. Her mother is deceased (or has gone to heaven, as Pippi puts it) and her father is a sea captain, sailing his ship on the seven seas. Pippi serves as an excellent model for young girls, and everyone else for that matter, who long to express opinions of their own and who refuse to bow to conventions and rules. For anyone who dreams of letting his fantasies loose, Pippi is a perfect idol. The Pippi in our book is actually an ordinary girl by the name of Hanna Lundström, and she has some similarities to the real Miss Longstocking: she is full of energy, smart and quick-witted, and she has a good sense of humour. But the story of our young heroine contains another ingredient: Hanna is the daughter of two parents who are both alive and present in her life and who divorced when she was considerably younger. Her sad mother has been left to manoeuvre her personal ship on her own. Her father has not been able to help his former wife, despite his well-intentioned but somewhat awkward efforts. If we take this background into consideration, Hanna's clinging to the idea that her father is a sea captain is a little bit too much. Her fantasies about his achievements develop into a rigid veneration of an idol.

The family romance and the divorce

Like many other children, Hanna has constructed for herself something which Sigmund Freud (1909b) named "the family romance", a concept that was further investigated by Kaplan (1974). Hanna is "actually" the daughter of a famous sea captain in Africa and her mother is an angel up in heaven. Why do many children make up such fantasies? Every child will discover, little by little, that his or her parents are not perfect. They will also notice that the adults in their life cannot always prevent them from feeling excluded, humiliated, angry and disappointed. The discovery of the imperfections in their parents and in adults generally can be saddening and disconcerting. The child reacts by creating a fantasy of actually having other parents than the real ones. These superparents are much nicer and more fun than Mum and Dad at home! The term "family romance" aims to describe this mechanism. For example, the child may fantasize about being an adopted child in his family. If only the king and queen would come and fetch him and take him back to the castle . . .

Family romances may become creative ingredients in children's play – if they assume reasonable proportions – but Hanna handles her fantasy in another way. She does not deny the fact that she has parents, but she maintains that in reality, her father is a sea captain and her mother is . . . Well, at this point she has a hard time struggling with defying reality. As a matter of fact, her mother is a sad presence in her life and Hanna is deeply concerned about her. Her father tries to help her to become more clear-sighted. He does not participate fully when she wants him to join her fantasy about his life as a sea captain. Concerning his love life, he persists in making it clear to Alma that he has a new partner, Beatrice. Similarly to Alma in Chapter 4, "Raging with love", and to many children in divorced families, Hanna finds it difficult to like her father's partner.

The problem with Beatrice is probably not that she is so "over the top" in her choice of eyeglasses, as Hanna expresses it. The painful thing is rather that she is not Hanna's mother. Nothing will ever change that. Furthermore, Hanna's mother is depressed, which adds another layer to the complication Hanna feels when she thinks about how much she loves her father. He is so kind but, nevertheless, he has abandoned Hanna's mother and found himself a new woman. Beatrice is not only an "intruder" but also a new and challenging acquaintance for the young girl. How will our Pippi be able to assemble this quadrangle?

Hanna's solution is to invent a father who is a devil of a fellow as a sea captain on the seven seas. On top of that, he and his daughter have something special in common! Pippi-Hanna is about to board her father's ship and to become his trusty shipmate, working together on the bridge! Beatrice will have to content herself with working below deck as a cook's helper in the galley. Obviously, we are into the passions of the Oedipus complex once again, the ones we discussed in the commentaries on Chapters 3 and 4, "Why are they doing like that?" and "Raging with love". The father tries to resist Hanna's fantasies and maintains that he is attending a sales meeting in Gothenburg. But he also allows himself to jest with his daughter and appoints her to be officer on board. Suddenly, Hanna's father is facing his personal problematic quadrangle. After all, what kind of job should he agree to offer Beatrice on board? The father has some obvious problems in relating to his daughter and to his new partner. In addition, he has a bad conscience towards his former wife, Hanna's mother. We get the impression that Mr Lundström is somewhat scared about navigating between all these reefs. Perhaps a dilemma such as his would deserve a chapter of its own . . .

Chapter 6 – You'll be deader than dead

Fantasy and reality

Ghosts, monsters and all kinds of frightening creatures enter the nursery. Selma Fraiberg (1987), an American child psychoanalyst, has described the ways in which these characters populate children's inner worlds. Typical for children is the fact that the borderline between internal and external characters is fluid. A child can easily convince herself that an imagined character is actually present in the external world. Such a process comes about in the following way: the imagined character, so to speak, leaves its internal home and the child "finds" it under the bed, in the wardrobe or in the darkest corner of her room. This is one of the reasons that children tend to be frightened of ghosts, tigers, darkness and insects, which we took up in our commentary on Chapter 2 about Bonnie, "The hole in the escalator". In Emma's case, in Chapter 6, these ghastly creatures moved out from her internal world and into her classmates, resulting in her becoming deeply frightened of Karen and all the other girls at school.

Emma created her characters in forms like "You-will-die" and "Emma-will-die". As long as she experienced them as external characters, they almost frightened her out of her senses. Analytic work was concentrated upon helping Emma differentiate between her fantasies and external reality. "Karen-you-will-die" was her fantasy, whereas Karen Nelson was the real classmate sitting next to her. It was equally important to help Emma understand the difference between thoughts and actions. Thinking "you-will-die" is not the same as killing your classmate.

Emma resumes contact with her analyst after four years. She is in a new phase of development, about to leave childhood and enter adolescence. She is also facing a conflict with her mother, and here we are talking about her real mother. Until now, she has been avoiding this conflict and protecting her mother and herself from facing it. Formerly, the character "Mother-will-die" was too scary to think about, but the time has come to deal with her. Emma needs to look into how angry she is with her mother's drinking and her evasive way of relating to Emma. Such a controversy is especially important to deal with now that Emma is nearly a teenager.

The adolescent will inevitably behave in an inconsistent and unpredictable manner. He is prone

> to fight his impulses and to accept them; to ward them off successfully and to be overrun by them; to love his parents and to hate them; to revolt against them and to be dependent on them; to be deeply ashamed to acknowledge his mother before others and, unexpectedly, to desire heart-to-heart talks with her; to thrive on imitation of and identification with others while searching unceasingly for his own identity; to be more idealistic, artistic, generous, and unselfish than he will ever be again, but also the opposite: self-centered, egoistic, calculating.
>
> (A. Freud, 1958, p. 275)

If the youngster manages to navigate reasonably well in these stormy waters, he will have a chance to turn development into positive directions (Blos, 1962) and to equip himself with better abilities for dealing with the passions of childhood. Such a positive development presupposes, however, that the teenager reorients himself vis-à-vis the parents. So far, Emma has not succeeded well in this project. She is stuck in a conflict with her mother, which has been swept under the carpet by the two of them. She is afraid to tackle it, and that prevents her from entering new and more exciting territories of adolescence.

In the beginning of this resumed contact, the analyst does not know what has caused Emma to be so terrified of dead people and skulls. Majlis assumes that Emma has resumed a pattern well known to her when she was younger: when she gets angry with someone, that person will die. For real! Such a method of dealing with anger is even less expedient today than during childhood. After all, now she is approaching the size and physical strength of the adults, such as her mother, and this frightens her. What if she were to beat up her mother next time she smells of wine?! Emma's entry into adolescence also implies that she must provide room for other adults: her parents, her peers and last but not least, Emma herself. Emma thus made a wise decision when she wanted to resume contact with her analyst. Her mother, whose concern for her daughter has always been apparent, was aware of Emma's needs and helped her to book an appointment with Majlis. The mother certainly also needs help in dealing with her issues. But that is another story . . .

Chapter 7 – We don't look into each other's eyes

We have emphasized the importance of attachment between mother and infant, as for example in our commentary on Chapter 2, "The hole in the escalator". The term "attachment" is often used today within the theoretical framework bearing its name. We refer to several comprehensive volumes (Bowlby, 1969, 1973, 1980; Cassidy & Shaver, 2008; Fonagy, 2001). To Bowlby, the term initially implied the young child's seeking of proximity in case of danger. In contrast, it did not refer to any influence by that which is so central to classic psychoanalytic theory – the drives. Today, the meaning of the concept has expanded to cover love relations between people of any age. In psychotherapeutic work with mother and infant, it is possible to study the very origins of attachment formation. Many prominent therapists have combined attachment theory with psychoanalytic theory in their work (e.g., Acquarone, 2004; Baradon et al., 2005; Daws, 1989; Fraiberg, 1980, 1987; Lebovici, 2000). We will soon acquaint ourselves with another technique that is based more consistently on a classical version of psychoanalytic theory – mother-infant psychoanalysis. Let us first, however, learn about a phenomenon described by one of the authors just mentioned, Selma Fraiberg.

The ghost in the nursery

Many therapy methods make use of a concept introduced by Selma Fraiberg and her colleagues (Fraiberg, Adelson & Shapiro, 1975): "the ghost in the nursery". We already know that little children tend to be afraid of ghosts, as exemplified by Bonnie in Chapter 2, "The hole in the escalator". The ghost in the nursery has another meaning; it refers to a parent's fear of his or her unconscious representations of the child. Since these ideas are unconscious, the parent finds it difficult to deal with them. As an example, we can consider a mother or a father who thinks that the child is a real crybaby. As soon as the child starts whining, the parent gets annoyed and compares the child to other children, who seem much happier and easier to deal with than this little crybaby. The parent says to him- or herself, "Something must be wrong with my child!" Our interpretation would rather be that the parent might harbour an unconscious fear of being a crybaby himself or herself. When the baby is crying, the "ghost" wakes up inside the parent, who does not know what to do with this crying he or she is faced with in the present. Nor does this parent know how to deal with his or her own past tendency to whine and cry, a tendency that perhaps has been repressed for decades. Now that one has become a parent, the baby's crying brings on feelings of anger and uselessness.

The parent might need help in understanding these feelings. The therapist might point out, "Do you notice that as soon as Charlie starts crying, you get annoyed? Perhaps he is not crying because he is a 'crybaby'. Might the issue rather be that his crying makes you feel tense and uncomfortable? How was it when you were little yourself and got sad or afraid?" In such situations, if the intervention is well-timed and reasonably accurate, the parent might respond, "I guess I'm a crybaby myself. At least I'm afraid of being one. I remember when I was a boy and my big brother used to tease me until I started crying. Then he would sob in imitation of me and tell me, 'Can't you see all the neighbours opening their windows? They wanna listen when you cry.'"

Mother-infant psychoanalysis

In the 1990s, the Swedish psychoanalyst Johan Norman (2001, 2004) introduced mother-infant psychoanalytic treatment, or MIP as it is often abbreviated. Rather than basing his method on attachment theory, he relied on classical and object relations psychoanalytic theory. Freud (1905) had already used an expression similar to attachment when describing the close contact between mother and infant: *die zärtliche Strömung*, which means "the affectionate current". Like Bowlby, the founder of the attachment concept, Freud assumed it serves the instinct of survival. Unlike Bowlby, however, Freud had theories about how the child becomes influenced from life's beginning by a sexual drive. The result was that an Unconscious was soon developed in the young mind (Salomonsson, 2012). Furthermore, Norman combined his reading of Freud with several ideas by Bion, notably the one of the importance of containing the baby's anxieties. Norman did this both indirectly, via a dialogue with the mother, and directly, via a "dialogue" with the baby. We refer to his case studies in the papers referenced, as well as to a recent monograph (Salomonsson, 2014).

This mode of therapy has now been evaluated systematically (Salomonsson & Sandell, 2011a, 2011b) in a randomized controlled trial (RCT). Compared with ordinary treatment at child health centres, MIP treatments demonstrated positive effects on the mother's depression, stress and sensitivity towards the child's communication. In addition, the relationships between the mother and infant developed in a more positive direction as compared with dyads undergoing ordinary treatment at the child health centres. These studies are summarized in the monograph mentioned earlier (Salomonsson, 2014). In MIP treatment, the analyst focuses on getting into a dialogue with the baby. Björn used this approach when Frida was screaming at the top of her lungs. He tried to describe to her the feelings that he assumed were raging inside her. He obviously did not believe that the baby understood the exact meaning of his words. He rather tried to interact with the child in order to make her feel contained (see Chapter 2, "The hole in the escalator"). When containment begins to work, it helps the child to express herself more clearly and to calm down.

In Frida's case, the analyst used ingredients from two sources: Fraiberg and Norman. Frida's mother and Björn talked about the fact that she was angry with him, but that she found it difficult to look into his eyes and speak with him. This problem was related to the mother's own "ghosts" from her childhood. When Frida started crying inconsolably, Björn tried to catch her attention. He tried to convey a message that Billie Holiday once expressed in a blues song: "Talk to me baby, tell me what's the matter now" (Salomonsson, 2007b). Of course, he did not expect that Frida would answer him verbally. His intention was rather to describe how she had felt forsaken by her mother. When this dialogue of the baby's screaming and the analyst's talking had been going on for ten intensive minutes, Frida started smiling. She had been allowed to cry out her pain to somebody who was prepared to listen to her with undivided attention. "Talk to me and I will listen carefully to you, Frida."

How are we to describe what Frida seemed to experience so intensely? The challenge of understanding that which the psychoanalyst W. R. Bion described as "O" is perhaps never greater than when one works with infants and parents. The analyst's ability to capture non-verbal signals is put to test, as is his or her imagination and intuition about what might be going on in the baby's mind. Bion would certainly have described Frida's panic as her "fear of dying" (1962). Infant researchers might describe it as the baby's difficulties with her affect regulation (Fonagy, Gergely, Jurist & Target, 2002). The latter term sounds more technical and scientific, whereas Bion's term sounds dramatic and perhaps unbelievable. How would a little creature be able to represent death? Bion was aware that our adult language is not well suited to describe a child's most painful feelings. But we would like to give it a try and translate Frida's panicky crying like this: "I am alone and forsaken. There is nobody out there who can explain to me what is happening, nobody to comfort me or cuddle me. I am about to break into pieces."

It is often enough for the crying baby to be picked up and put on Mum's lap in order to be transformed into a curious and happy little one. The child has now resumed contact with the mother's containment. The attachment has been secured by the mother's lifting her child up and naming her feelings. She might do this by simply saying words like, "Now little one, what's the matter?" Perhaps we might translate this little sentence into, "Little one, you think you are alone but I am by your side. You think you are succumbing, but you are still living and you will go on living and so will I. What is happening now is not dangerous. Yes, I know it has happened before and it will happen again. Every time it happens, I will do my best to be with you and take care of you." Of course, no parent actually speaks that way to the child. Our translation seeks to capture what we think helps the baby to become calm again: the mother's hope, care, attention, patience and love. She conveys all of this, not only through her words but also through her tone of voice and posture when holding her child. It is a daily miracle.

Chapter 8 – My head is a mess

Neuropsychiatry – a never-ending debate

ADHD (attention deficit/hyperactivity disorder) and DAMP (deficits in attention, motor control and perception) are two diagnoses that have caused bitter discussions with strong reactions and counter-reactions. To put it simply, we might say that two factions are opposing each other. One of them claims that ADHD is a neuropsychiatric disturbance caused by genetic and biological factors. Treatment should therefore be pharmacological and pedagogical. It ought to focus on behavioural changes, not on psychotherapy. The other faction maintains that ADHD is caused by changes in society that have caused children to feel more and more stressed. According to this faction, the focus should be on dealing with these changes in society, rather than letting them remain concealed by treating symptoms with pharmacological drugs.

We take a third position. Once we have clarified the diagnostic concepts, the problem will retain its complexity but we will be able to come out of the thicket of the debate. As many authors have asserted, ADHD is a diagnosis describing a number of symptoms and nothing else. As a matter of fact, this applies to most psychiatric diagnoses; they subsume a number of symptoms, whereas they say nothing about what has caused them to appear. The ADHD diagnosis of Noah says nothing about whether his behaviour is caused by non-optimal genes, defective enzymes in his brain or environmental factors in the family or in society. His diagnosis merely describes that he is hyperactive and impulsive and has difficulties in concentrating. Neither does it tell us anything about Noah's "Land of O", because this term refers to a genuinely individual place that can be investigated only in a personal encounter with his therapist. Unfortunately, we see today how the implications of an ADHD diagnosis are sliding. Nowadays many people tend to regard it as identical to a biological dysfunction, despite the fact that modern psychiatric diagnoses do not contain any causal formulations. As we see it, this sliding in the interpretation of ADHD marks an unfortunate development, both for the treatment of the child and for the clarity of the discourse (Salomonsson, 2004, 2006, 2011).

ADHD and emotions

A psychoanalyst cannot establish the causes behind a child's ADHD symptoms. What he can do, however, is to help the individual child to learn to express his feelings in a more comprehensible way than by fighting or just running about. It is sometimes claimed that ADHD symptoms are not in any primary way related to emotions. In Noah's case, such a position would imply that he cannot sit still in his chair owing to a dysfunction of his brain. This position further presupposes that any other symptoms are secondary reactions to the annoyance or even scorn that people around him show when he is restless and troublesome. Their reactions make him feel angry and humiliated. We would like to put forth a different position based on our experiences: when the analyst together with the child tries to map out an impulsive act, we often find that the child is actually harbouring a painful emotion. This emotion is trying to surge through the surface, but the child does not want to acknowledge its existence. He rather tries to get rid of the feeling through an impulsive act or hyperactivity, leading him to become rowdy and to start a quarrel.

If we ask a child, "What are you feeling?" we often get the answer "nothing", followed by the child's shrugging his shoulders. This was the case between Björn and Noah. In order to reflect on such a question, the child needs access to "an alphabet of emotions". He needs help to identify feelings like "happy", "annoyed", "pissed off" and so forth. He also needs to learn that such emotions are not dangerous per se. What might cause trouble, however, is the inability to handle the consequences of these emotions. This implies that the results of a psychoanalytic treatment with children like Noah may vary. It is not always certain that hyperactivity itself will vanish. There are preliminary results in this direction from a German psychotherapy study with children (Leuzinger-Bohleber & Fischmann, 2010). Where psychotherapy does seem to be more consistently efficacious is with regard to the child's emotional troubles. It can help him become more "agile" in expressing what he is feeling, instead of letting his impulses take over. Noah's conversation with Ken indicates that he is about to master the art of having an emotion without letting it govern him. This can lead him to feel less anxious and depressed, a pattern also indicated by the German study mentioned earlier.

There is an increasing number of papers dealing with psychoanalytic therapy for children with ADHD (Eresund, 2007; Gensler, 2011; Gilmore, 2000; Günter, 2013; Rainwater, 2007; Sugarman, 2006). Some focus on these children's often disturbed relationships with other people. Others focus on technique, believing that the child's problems in symbolizing his emotions and experiences make it important for the therapist to gauge his interventions carefully. Otherwise the therapist runs the risk that the child will experience his words as an attack or criticism, rather than vehicles for his intention to help the child.

The treatment of ADHD

We would like to emphasize, in accordance with most professionals treating children with an ADHD diagnosis, the need for creating calm environments for them at preschool and school with small groups of children and a consistent team of educators. Big and hectic milieus easily trigger hyperactivity and impulsivity. The child finds it hard to filter sensorial impressions and cannot focus on the tasks at school. The analyst also needs to bear this difficulty in mind. It is important not to heap a mass of words upon the child, however wise and relevant these words might be. They need to be portioned out at a pace which the child can manage.

Concerning medication with central stimulants, it has often been put in opposition to psychotherapy, at least in the public debate. The opponents to psychopharmacology claim that the drugs are used to silence the child's feelings. In contrast, people who recommend central stimulants claim that this treatment is the one which has received the most solid scientific support (Barkley, 2006). According to our experience, medication is indeed sometimes needed as a complement to other sorts of treatment. Its aim is to help the child "collect himself". This does not stand in any logical opposition to the goals of psychotherapy. In some cases, the dampening of hyperactivity brought about by medication may make the child more accessible to psychotherapeutic interventions. Nevertheless, we think drugs are sometimes prescribed in an uncritical way. Our main objection concerns the cases when a child is offered drugs without simultaneously being considered for psychotherapy. Most children of today have therefore not been offered the experience of sorting things out when they feel, like Noah did, that "my head is a mess". We find this highly unsatisfactory. One may ask, in line with the title of a paper by Zabarenko (2011), why haven't we psychoanalysts, neuroscientists and cognitive psychologists fielded a team to further our understanding of the genesis, symptoms and treatment of this increasingly frequent disorder?

Chapter 9 – Restless and ruthless – or just rootless?

In Hollywood movies and TV series the hero is strong, handsome and clever. In contrast, the heroes of the Bible are human beings who often have quite a few tiresome or even unsympathetic qualities. Moses in the Bible is a man of great principles who is willing to make far-reaching sacrifices to the benefit of his people. He is also said to be a patient man. However, he can sometimes be stern and uncompromising. Concerning his patience, well, it is not always one of his most prominent character traits. Our story is a mixture of tales from the books of Exodus and Numbers and some fantasies about the mother of Moses. We focus on how she might have experienced her delivery and the time immediately following it, known from the famous story of Moses in the reed basket. We combine our interpretation of these events with the descriptions of Moses in Egypt and later in the desert, such as his propensity to become enraged and violent (Exodus 2:12).

In our imagination, Moses has not succeeded in entering through "the locked door", which he has experienced when being with his mother. His pain and sense of exclusion have led him to feel a heightened sense of anxiety and have left him with a tendency to substitute actions for thinking. Thus, a vicious circle is created of impulsivity, negative reactions from the environment, new outbreaks from Moses and so on. In that way, Moses reminds us of young Noah in Chapter 8, "My head is a mess."

Traumatized parents and their children

Parents of impulsive children often feel burdened with guilt and remorse stemming from the judgemental attitudes of people around them. However, extreme circumstances of life are not infrequently a significant part of the picture. Every day, we read or hear news about parents being threatened by violence and humiliations. We thus know that Moses's mother has many "kindred spirits" in many countries all over the world. Even in the modern Western world, women may be abandoned and may feel helpless in a number of other ways. The psychologist and researcher Atia Daud (2008) recently showed that children of traumatized parents can become severely affected. He found associations between post-traumatic stress syndromes among parents and ADHD symptoms among their children. The trauma thus seems to have continued within the child, despite the parents' attempts to prevent such a development. Many parents worry that their child is impulsive or hyperactive, or that he or she seems anxious or agitated. Such children ought to receive help as soon as possible. Little Moses and his successors today need a qualified treatment that is instituted early. We regard psychotherapy as an often important ingredient for children who have suffered trauma. Many psychoanalytic papers discuss the trauma concept and also illustrate childhood trauma through clinical examples (Chertoff, 2009; Gaensbauer, 1995, 2011; Lieberman & Harris, 2007; Marans, 2008).

One final comment: we hope that our tales of Moses's hot temper and Noah's rowdiness have not created a false notion that traumatized children are primarily a pest and a nuisance. Our stories about Moses and Noah indicate that their impulsivity and hot temper join hands with excellent human qualities: a passion for justice, a sense of leadership and an ability to express themselves clearly and loudly when such qualities are called for. Psychotherapy should certainly not aim at doing away with such qualities but rather help the child master the suffering that lingers on long after the traumatizing event.

Chapter 10 – Letter from the volcano

In the commentary on Chapter 3, "Why are they doing like that?" we wrote that the analyst's personal feelings vis-à-vis Peter were an important tool for understanding the boy. We then introduced the concept of countertransference, and now it is time to examine it somewhat more deeply. We previously defined it briefly, saying that countertransference is the sum total of the analyst's feelings and fantasies towards his patient. It is not important whether these feelings and fantasies are positive or negative, but rather that they exist and that they are taken into account in the analyst's thinking. It is only when the analyst does not notice his countertransference that it might become an obstacle. In that case he might be ruled by it and put it into action. In contrast, if he is able to use it in an optimal way, it may serve as a tool and a guide forward in treatment. While working with Linda, the analyst noticed that he felt excluded by a ten-year-old girl, who was sitting with her drawings in a most calm and polite manner. It was even more stupefying when he noticed that he was indulging in fantasies about making a luminous career. If he had transformed his fantasies into actions he might, for example, have become sarcastic towards Linda or uninterested in her. He took another position: quietly, he reflected on his feelings and on what they might have to do with Linda. It might be objected that the analyst was ambitious, and that this simply had nothing to do with Linda. But he interpreted his feelings in another way: as an expression of his countertransference towards her.

Transference

In order to better understand the concept of countertransference, we must start with the concept of transference. The patient is not aware of all the fantasies and feelings hiding behind his or her emotional suffering. Instead, he *transfers* them onto his analyst. He might experience the analyst as rejecting and harsh, sensual and enticing, greedy and inaccessible or nice and understanding. Obviously, the options are endless. To be sure, the analyst might actually have one or more of the personality traits ascribed to him. The concept of transference, however, refers to experiences that the patient has had with his loved ones at some time in his life. In the therapeutic encounter, he "reads" them into his analyst. According to Freud, patients are especially bound to transfer representations and feelings stemming from early childhood.

Anyone who has been in therapy has probably noticed a tendency to experience the therapist in an exaggerated and emotional manner. One example is seen when Peter (in Chapter 3, "Why are they doing like that?") gets angry with the therapist because he is on the phone one minute before letting Peter come into his office. With the "adult" aspect of his personality, Peter is well aware that one minute will pass quickly and that the therapist will certainly open the door soon. But according to the "childish" facet of his personality, one minute implies eternity. He might get the idea that Björn is on the phone because he does not care about him, or because Björn wants to punish Peter for having been nasty earlier. Such an idea is called transference. Perhaps Peter has experienced earlier in his life that adults have tended to treat him that way. Feelings, attitudes and fantasies of such kinds usually vary during the course of treatment. Last but not least, transference occurs in every patient in therapy regardless of gender, age, education or knowledge about psychotherapy.

We also would like to illustrate transference with the views many of us had about our teachers, back in our school years. Today, we probably realize that they were not as terrible or wonderful, ugly or beautiful, harsh or brilliant as we tended to imagine then. Rather, we were imposing our childish fantasies about the adult world, sometimes mixed with some accurate and astute observations, on our teachers. Thus was born the teenager's contempt for his maths teacher, as well as the young schoolboy's passion for his beautiful art teacher. There are other people who also tend to become transference objects, such as musicians, politicians and, not least, our partners.

Countertransference – II

If we now return to the concept of countertransference, we realize that it is the mirror image of transference. It is the analyst's emotional response to the patient's transference. Freud emphasized that countertransference applies above all to the patient's impact on the analyst's *unconscious* feelings. He insisted that the analyst should recognize this countertransference and master it. His stance here seems surprisingly strict, but Freud was aware of the strong forces that are set in motion by psychoanalysis. A psychoanalyst who is not aware of when he becomes delighted, annoyed or jealous through the influence of his patient is, of course, unable to do a good job.

Today, countertransference is still regarded as an awkward and personal obstacle for the analyst – but only sometimes! In such cases, we have to handle it, either by resuming our personal psychoanalysis or by seeking supervision. However, and this is important for anyone who seeks to understand present-day scientific discussions within psychoanalysis, we also regard countertransference as a creative possibility for understanding the patient. It is more and more regarded as something which needs to be worked through (Pick, 1985) internally by the analyst. Contemporary psychoanalysis thus focuses more and more on the *interaction* between patient and analyst. For an exhaustive discussion of how the countertransference concept has evolved over the years, we refer to an interesting monograph (Brown, 2011). If we get back to young Linda, she will probably always harbour a tiny and weak facet in her personality. But her interaction with the analyst helped her to become more "agile" or at ease in dealing with it. Had the analyst become afraid of his countertransference, he might have become rigid instead. Treatment would then have been changed into his lecturing to her about her behaviour. Such a stance would have contributed to making Linda even more anxious about the sides of herself that cause her to feel pitiful and ashamed.

Psychoanalytic treatment often involves a highly intense interaction with a patient, which calls for sincerity on the part of the analyst, not least towards himself. This sincerity can be formulated as a resolve to approach his own Land of O. Needless to say, this task can be daunting and embarrassing. He ought to pay attention to the fact that he is becoming absorbed in thoughts of career-ladder climbing while he is being excluded by a ten-year-old girl – and he should also reflect on why this occurs. If he assumes that his ambitious thoughts relate to his private personal situation, he will have to deal with that issue himself. But if he thinks that these thoughts can tell him something about his interaction with Linda and about *her* Land of O, then he should try to understand what is going on – within her and between the two of them.

When Linda told him how sad she was standing inside the monkey area and not being allowed by the other children to come out, the analyst was reminded of similar feelings when he was standing in the schoolyard during his childhood. Heinz Racker (1968) called such a phenomenon "concordant" countertransference. In other situations, countertransference might be "complementary", meaning that the analyst's emotions link into the patient's unconscious emotions, somewhat like two cogwheels rotating together. This occurred when the analyst fantasized that he was powerful and famous, a position in stark contrast to the little excluded child that Linda was denying inside herself. In that way, the mighty analyst and the little excluded Linda became two complementary characters.

The art of being a psychotherapist is to allow oneself to be moved by such emotions but not to act them out. It is easy to be uncomfortable about feeling tiny and powerless. Similarly, it is natural for the therapist to feel guilty when he aims to help a young girl achieve a better self-esteem, but instead finds himself fantasizing about becoming famous. However, his observations of his discomfort and guilt may be used in order to understand what is going on inside the patient. Moreover, the therapist's analysis of countertransference is often the very foundation of psychotherapeutic work. In that way, such work is for the most part highly rewarding and stimulating. It can seem to come to a standstill on occasions, but it is never uninteresting. When one works with children, another component is added – namely, that they tend to interact physically with the therapist. Furthermore, they tend to awaken the analyst's personal feelings from his or her childhood. Therefore, countertransference is often more intense than when one works with adult patients. We refer to volumes by Tsiantis, Sandler and Martindale (1996) and Blake (2008).

Chapter 11 – That tingling feeling

Ronia is one of the most beloved of the many child characters created by the Swedish author Astrid Lindgren. She is an open-minded and wild tomboy who rides her horse bareback in the forest. In springtime, when trees are budding and migrant birds are returning from warmer countries, she releases a loud shout of joy that she calls her great spring-scream.

The book's description of her transformation – from a candid young girl to a bewildered and questioning teenager – is a fascinating description of a young girl's development.

Body and soul – everything is changing

The first signs of transformation during puberty occur in the body. Girls start having their periods and their breasts start developing. We can say that the tingling feelings within Ronia reposition themselves in her young body. She recalls a time when her tingling feelings were linked to childhood masturbatory activities. Similar feelings probably also touched little Alma in Chapter 4, "Raging with love", when she discovered the newcomer in her neighbourhood, young Dawit. But Ronia has reached much further in her development and is now on her way to becoming a young woman. She discovers new phenomena in herself, in which emotional and bodily changes run parallel. It is as if she goes from hot to cold and back to hot again, all over her body and all the time. Her budding love for Birk begins with childish games and contests. But soon, the two become attached to one another in a new and unfamiliar way, a development which has consequences on different levels.

No one in the stronghold can ignore Ronia's changes. When her father, Matt, discovers the love between Ronia and Birk, he is enraged and devastated. His reaction expresses his anger at the young boy's father, Borka, who happens to be his long-time arch-rival. But it also testifies to a father's difficulties in letting his daughter go away with a whippersnapper like Birk to Borka's Keep on the other side of Hell's Gap. Once again, we become acquainted with the Oedipus complex, now within a family of crooks and robbers. Ronia feels a need to pull away from her parents in order to find her own way. She has started to look with new and questioning eyes upon her mother, Lovis, and her father, Matt, who up until now have been the most central and self-evident people in her life.

The parents – bonds and liberation

The young adolescent needs to reassess the relationship with her parents. Old bonds need to be dissolved. Winnicott (1971) insisted that this liberation presupposes that the young person "murders" the internal idealized parent. At the same time, the real parent must survive the teenager's attack. Winnicott did not hesitate to use powerful expressions when showing that the teenager's struggle to carve out and live a life of her own is a struggle of life and death. The teenager is, of course, afraid, even terrified, of harming the parents for real. However, refraining from such efforts at liberation will make development come to a halt. The teenager will never release herself from the bonds of childhood but will instead remain in an immature dependence. If Ronia were to refrain from setting herself free, she would eternally worship her strong, brave and fabulous father. But once she begins to liberate herself from her parents, she fears she will succumb in a dangerous world. That would imply that Ronia would never be able to return to Matt's stronghold, and right now she cannot imagine such a catastrophe. In the end, she resorts to a hopeful fantasy: maybe one day she'll dare tell her father what she thinks about his bragging and his manners.

What happens when these bonds towards the parents are untied? They might be directed towards the child's self. Let us demonstrate with an adolescent who spends his entire days in front of his computer, playing games. He seems to have released himself from his parents. "DO NOT ENTER" is written on the door to his room. But silently, he might be preoccupied with an intense dialogue with his internal fantasy-parents. Alternatively, he might seek to retie the old bonds but to other people – for example, teachers or other adults or idols. Suddenly, the gym teacher seems infinitely smarter and more interesting than old Dad, who can have a hard time accepting this displacement!

The old bonds may also take another direction – towards the teenager's friends. He can identify with them – or hide among them. The group is a place of free experimentation without any demands, at least up to a certain point. This applies to an even greater extent to the teenager's love relationships. He may mix the passions of childhood with the sexual cravings of youth. One minute, the teenager and his girlfriend are giggling at trivial matters, and the next they are having serious deliberations on how many children to have when they become adults. Or, they take an even deeper view and ponder on the entire meaning of life. In the end, the adult love relationship will have to find room for all these great or trivial debates. It is no wonder that teenagers sometimes have immense difficulties in finding the Right One!

Ronia cannot share all these new discoveries about herself, her body and her feelings with her father. To an even lesser extent can she share them with the robbers in the stronghold. She is not even able to go to her mother, Lovis, and talk about all these new things inside and outside of her young person. She is left alone with her thoughts and preoccupations about herself. Then she comes to think of Birk. Maybe she should have a talk with him? Would Birk listen to her? Our story ends here and leaves the answer to our imagination . . .

Chapter 12 – No connection

What makes it such a catastrophe for Maya when she is staying at the countryside cabin with her mother and Craig? She blames it on the fact that she has no connection to the Internet and that she cannot rely on her cell phone. As the hours pass by, she notices something spooky. Until now, she has thought that communication means being connected to the external world. As long as she is connected to the Internet, she is in contact and communicates with people. However, her brief stay at the countryside cabin forces her to discover something else. She begins to communicate with herself in a new way, instead of up- and downloading pics with all her Facebook friends.

Maya discovers a new kind of connection: not with the outside world but with her innermost world of feelings and thoughts. She notices that her grandfather's death from lung cancer is more present in her mind than she had been thinking. When she connects to other thoughts inside, she discovers many more feelings. She misses her grandmother and is afraid of the dark attic. She remembers being shy with the young man she met briefly in Uppsala. Maya experiences herself standing in-between connections: outwards and inwards. In the family's countryside cabin the link outward, the Internet connection, does not function. This "catastrophe" pushes her to discovering the connections inwards. In other words, she is getting closer to her Land of O.

This oscillation between experiencing the external and internal worlds is typical for adolescents. They visit the internal world and they like it for a while, but suddenly it gets scary and they feel like they never want to visit it again. They rush out, slam the door and develop different defensive manoeuvres. Typical for Maya are her almost manic efforts to re-establish the connections outwards. When she discovers that the Internet connection does not work, her defence mechanism capsizes. We guess this is the main reason that she gets scared when she arrives with Mum and Craig to the cabin and discovers the empty screen blinking "no network". Why does she think that everything is dead now, that life is meaningless and empty without the Web? We guess it is because her connections inwards are starting to make themselves known. All the many strange feelings that she otherwise tends to disregard are now popping up. Her response is typical for adolescents; she turns to Eleanor, a girl of her own age, and implores her, "Promise me that you don't believe I've become childish."

What Maya does *not* know is that Eleanor is struggling with a similar fear of becoming a child again. Perhaps it dawns on Maya as Eleanor reveals, in her second letter, the details of her Barbie game and deliberations about her previous issues with eating. Once again, we see the enormous help that the teenager may get from a close friend; she makes you realize that you are not as lonely in the universe as you sometimes think. During their correspondence, the two girls discover that such fellowship needs no modems or Internet servers. It needs the courage to be trustful and confident in one's friend. Finally, as we have mentioned eating disorders, anyone interested in a psychoanalytic perspective on this condition might consult a volume by Lawrence (2008).

Adolescent sexuality

It is not until the noise of the external world has quieted down that Maya becomes conscious of her thoughts and feelings about childhood, death and other scary things. All these thoughts are frightening but also enticing and interesting. What themes occupy young people's minds and feelings? The typical and spontaneous answer to this question is, of course, sexuality. We know that teenagers today are well informed and have more freedom than ever to explore their sexuality. They discuss, in an open and frank way, topics like venereal diseases, condoms and HIV. But, paradoxically, other aspects of sexuality are not as conscious and easy to talk about, owing to the teenager's embarrassment about them. One example is Maya's feelings for the young man in Uppsala. What embarrasses her is not the fact that he is good-looking or that she is in love with him. It is rather that Maya feels so small and vulnerable and in danger of being dependent when she thinks of him. The great catastrophe she fears is that her fantasies about him will drag her down into the helplessness of her childhood. Better get back quickly to becoming that cool girl constantly surfing on the Web!

Ronia, in Chapter 11, "That tingling feeling", is struggling with the same questions. Should she dare to fall in love? Should she dare to show her feelings to Birk? In one aspect, Maya has proceeded further than Ronia. She has started seeing boys and she is also older than Astrid Lindgren's storybook character. But, in a way, Ronia is braver than Maya. She is thinking about talking to Birk about her feelings. Maya is shyer and wants to reassure herself that her friend Eleanor will never tell anybody about the feelings she has confided.

Building a new identity

Maya's task in life at this point is to become independent vis-à-vis her parents *and* to build up a relationship with a boy whom she can trust and depend on, and with whom she can discuss the great questions that beset a young person: "Who am I? Who do I want to be?" In other words, her task is one of building a new identity, which is a vital issue for all teenagers. The concept of identity is far from being restricted to psychoanalytic writings. It is, in fact, a complex and abstruse concept. Anyone interested in getting acquainted with psychoanalytic perspectives on "adolescent identities" (note the plural!) is referred to a volume edited by Browning (2008a). Identity may simply be defined as the essence of how one experiences oneself. We regard identity as the ongoing and personal structuring and consolidating project of the teenager. It could also be described as the experience of being someone and of being oneself. Simply speaking, our identity is the linchpin of our personality.

The teenager can "inhabit" her identity, and she can see it as a place where she can shield herself from two major threats encountered in this stage of development. One of them is the youngster's helplessness and childish dependence, those embarrassing impulses that could drag her into the world of childhood once again. The other threat is the temptation to cut the bonds with her parents too quickly and too categorically and then develop into an "as-if adult". The road to building an identity is obviously long and complicated. No wonder teenagers can seem so lost and bewildered! They are restless and active and then, all of a sudden, they isolate themselves and seem overcome with ennui. One second, Maya thinks her mother's suggestion to write a letter to Eleanor is utterly ridiculous. The next second, she writes that very letter! The rapid shifts make it hard for the adult world at school and at home to understand teenagers. On top of it all, it is only rarely that the teenager herself understands what is going on inside her.

Identity is not a construction that is erected once and for all and then remains unchanged. It rather develops as the individual advances in maturity and gathers personal experiences. At the same time, if identity is being developed in isolation we have good reasons to feel worried. The teenager must interact with others and must be influenced by them – otherwise she becomes a solipsistic and isolated character with a stunted identity. Accordingly, adolescents feel like they must have endless chats about anything whatsoever with anybody whomsoever. Like Maya, teenagers also need a best friend to rely on and to be understood and mirrored by. Maya and Eleanor talk about everything. But, if we listen carefully, we notice that the traffic is often one-way. Its purpose is often to find a way of expressing one's own feelings and thoughts rather than listening to the friend. Furthermore, both Maya and Eleanor tend to prefer talking about connecting outwards to connecting inwards. It is scary to get too personal even with your best friend. On the other hand, it is easy to see development in the two girls' correspondence. They change, from spuriously agreeing that life with no Internet connection is worthless to cautiously sharing several personal and embarrassing secrets.

Many youngsters use the Web in order to seek out their identity or identities. The Internet is the playground of our century. Many children and youngsters are being looked after intensively by the school and their parents. But on the Internet they can play about in a more free and undisturbed manner. Understandably, many parents worry about this development. Surfing on the Web entails risks. Teenagers may be misused and maltreated. We are aware of the risks with this modern mode of communication. And, as we have illustrated in the sequence about Maya, she tends to use the Internet to protect herself from being alone with her innermost feelings and thoughts.

At the same time, the Internet also has a great potential to help youngsters in their personal development. Let us illustrate our idea with a youngster who is struggling with a suspicion that he is homosexual. He has heard from his teacher in biology that this is a normal phenomenon. He knows of a lot of celebrities who have "come out" and told the world they are gay. But this knowledge does not prevent him from being afraid. Furthermore, he does not want to talk about his feelings with anybody close to him. Instead, he connects himself to the Internet and chats anonymously with other youngsters. There he finds a possibility of getting answers about the great questions that might lie behind his worries. Maybe his main concern is not about his sexual orientation but about whether he can feel secure as a man. Is he the only one who has such thoughts or are there other guys who ponder about similar things? Here, the Internet might help him feel less lonely and strengthen his identity of being as much of an ordinary fellow as anyone else. This way, his connection outwards to the Internet enables him to connect inwards, to his innermost feelings.

Psychotherapy with teenagers presents special problems. Anna Freud once said (quoted by Geleerd, 1957), "One cannot analyze in adolescence. It is like running next to an express train." Today we think differently. It is not quite as impossible as it might seem. However, the therapist needs to mobilize a lot of patience, humour, tolerance and spontaneity. He or she also needs to be prepared for strong emotional shifts in the young patient's feelings and motivations to remain in therapy. It is good to bear in mind something that Donald Meltzer once told us: that the goals of adolescent psychoanalysis may not always be a full-scale analysis of the neurotic conflict. Instead, we often have to content ourselves with what he called "a slice of psychoanalysis". One day, the future adult may come back to his analyst and ask for a second slice, and perhaps a bigger one at that. Many works have been written on psychoanalysis and psychotherapy in adolescence (Anderson & Dartington, 1998; Browning, 2008b; Laufer, 1997; Laufer & Laufer, 1984; Perret-Catipovic & Ladame, 1998). The psychoanalytic classic is a book by Peter Blos, *On Adolescence* (1962).

Our letters and commentaries have passed through two decades of human development. We began by describing the first acts of relating through looking into Mother's eyes, and we ended by portraying the agonies when a youngster is about to leave the parents to carve out an existence of one's own in young adulthood. If our commentaries seemed brief, we apologize by explaining that they were written in order to whet the reader's appetite for further reflection and reading. We refer to the reference list for anyone who wishes to deepen his or her interest in these fascinating areas.

References

Acquarone, S. (2004). *Infant-parent psychotherapy*. London: Karnac Books.
Allwood, M. (Ed.). (1983). *Modern Swedish poetry*. Mullsjö: Anglo-American Center.
Anderson, R., & Dartington, A. (Eds.). (1998). *Facing it out: Clinical perspectives on adolescent disturbance*. London: Duckworth.
Badoni, M. (2002). Parents and their child and the analyst in the middle. *International Journal of Psychoanalysis, 83*(5), 1111–1131.
Balter, L., Lothane, Z., & Spencer, J. H. (1980). On the analyzing instrument. *Psychoanalytic Quarterly, 49*, 475–503.
Baradon, T., Broughton, C., Gibbs, I., James, J., Joyce, A., & Woodhead, J. (2005). *The practice of psychoanalytic parent-infant psychotherapy – Claiming the baby*. London: Routledge.
Barkley, R. A. (2006). *Attention-deficit hyperactivity disorder* (3rd ed.). New York, NY: Guilford Press.
Beck, C. T., & Indman, P. (2005). The many faces of postpartum depression. *Journal of Obstetric, Gynecologic, & Neonatal Nursing, 34*(5), 569–576.
Bion, W. R. (1962). *Learning from experience*. London: Karnac Books.
Bion, W. R. (1965). *Transformations*. London: Karnac Books.
Bion, W. R. (1970). *Attention and interpretation*. London: Karnac Books.
Blake, P. (2008). *Child and adolescent psychotherapy*. London: Karnac Books.
Bleger, J. (1967). Psychoanalysis of the psychoanalytic frame. *International Journal of Psychoanalysis, 48*, 511–519.
Blos, P. (1962). *On adolescence: A psychoanalytic interpretation*. London: Free Association Press.
Bornstein, B. (1949). The analysis of a phobic child – Some problems of theory and technique in child analysis. *Psychoanalytic Study of the Child, 3*, 181–226.
Bowlby, J. (1969). *Attachment and loss*. London: Pimlico.
Bowlby, J. (1973). *Separation: Anger and anxiety*. London: Pimlico.
Bowlby, J. (1980). *Loss: Sadness and depression*. London: Pimlico.
Brown, L. J. (2011). *Intersubjective processes and the Unconscious*. London: Routledge.
Browning, D. L. (Ed.). (2008a). *Adolescent identities*. New York, NY: Analytic Press.

References

Browning, D. L. (Ed.). (2008b). *Adolescent readings: A collection of readings.* New York, NY: Analytic Press.

Camus, A. (1994). *Le premier homme (The first man).* Paris: Gallimard (Engl. ed.: New York: Vintage International, 1996, translated by D. Hapgood).

Cassidy, J., & Shaver, P. R. (2008). *Handbook of attachment: Theory, research, and clinical applications* (2nd ed.). New York, NY: Guilford Press.

Chertoff, J. M. (2009). The complex nature of exposure to early childhood trauma in the psychoanalysis of a child. *Journal of the American Psychoanalytic Association, 57*, 1425–1457.

Cohen, P. (1989). Reconstruction of a germ phobia in a latency girl. *Bulletin of the Anna Freud Centre, 12*, 281–295.

Daud, A. (2008). *Post-traumatic stress disorder and resilience in children of traumatised parents: A transgenerational perspective.* Stockholm: Karolinska Institutet.

Daws, D. (1989). *Through the night: Helping parents and sleepless infants.* New York, NY: Basic Books.

Dowd Stone, S., & Menken, A. (Eds.). (2008). *Perinatal and postpartum mood disorders: Perspectives and treatment guide for the health practitioner.* New York, NY: Springer.

Ekelöf, G. (1965). *Dikter (Poems).* Stockholm: Bonniers.

Eresund, P. (2007). Psychodynamic psychotherapy for children with disruptive disorders. *Journal of Child Psychotherapy, 33*(2), 161–180.

Field, T. (2010). Postpartum depression effects on early interactions, parenting, and safety practices: A review. *Infant Behavior & Development, 33*(1), 1–6.

Field, T., Healy, B., Goldstein, S., Perry, S., Bendell, D., Schanberg, S., . . . Kuhn, C. (1988). Infants of depressed mothers show "depressed" behavior even with nondepressed adults. *Child Development, 59*(6), 1569–1579.

Field, T., Hernandez-Reif, M., Diego, M., Feijo, L., Vera, Y., Gil, K., & Sanders, C. (2007). Still-face and separation effects on depressed mother-infant interactions. *Infant Mental Health Journal, 28*(3), 314–323.

Fonagy, P. (2001). *Attachment theory and psychoanalysis.* New York, NY: Other Press.

Fonagy, P., Gergely, G., Jurist, E. L., & Target, M. (2002). *Affect regulation, mentalization, and the development of the self.* New York, NY: Other Press.

Fraiberg, S. (1980). *Clinical studies in infant mental health.* New York, NY: Basic Books.

Fraiberg, S. (1987). *Selected writings of Selma Fraiberg.* Columbus, OH: Ohio State University Press.

Fraiberg, S., Adelson, E., & Shapiro, V. (1975). Ghosts in the nursery. A psychoanalytic approach to the problems of impaired infant-mother relationships. *Journal of the American Academy of Child Psychiatry, 14*(3), 387–421.

Freud, A. (1926). *Introduction to the technique of child analysis.* London: Imago.

Freud, A. (1958). Adolescence. *Psychoanalytic Study of the Child, 13*, 255–278.

Freud, A. (1965). *Normality and pathology in childhood: Assessments of development.* New York, NY: International Universities Press.

Freud, S. (1900). The interpretation of dreams. *The standard edition of the complete psychological works of Sigmund Freud (SE*, Vol. 4–5). London: Hogarth Press.

References

Freud, S. (1905). Three essays on sexuality. *SE* (Vol. 7, pp. 123–246).
Freud, S. (1909a). Analysis of a phobia in a five-year-old boy. *SE* (Vol. 10, pp. 1–150).
Freud, S. (1909b). Family romances. *SE* (Vol. 9, pp. 235–242).
Gaensbauer, T. (1995). Trauma in the preverbal period: Symptoms, memories, and developmental impact. *Psychoanalytic Study of the Child, 50*, 122–149.
Gaensbauer, T. (2011). Embodied simulation, mirror neurons, and the reenactment of trauma in early childhood. *Neuropsychoanalysis, 13*(1), 91–107.
Geleerd, E. R. (1957). Some aspects of psychoanalytic technique in adolescence. *Psychoanalytic Study of the Child, 12*, 263–283.
Gensler, D. (2011). Trouble paying attention. *Journal of Infant, Child & Adolescent Psychotherapy, 10*, 103–115.
Gilmore, K. (2000). A psychoanalytic perspective on attention-deficit/hyperactivity disorder. *Journal of the American Psychoanalytic Association, 48*(4), 1259–1293.
Goodman, S. H. (2007). Depression in mothers. *Annual Review of Clinical Psychology, 3*, 107–135.
Grotstein, J. S. (1990). Nothingness, meaninglessness, chaos, and the "black hole" II. *Contemporary Psychoanalysis, 26*, 377–407.
Grotstein, J. S. (2008). *A beam of intense darkness: Wilfred Bion's legacy to psychoanalysis*. London: Karnac Books.
Günter, M. (2013). Attention deficit hyperactivity disorder (ADHD): An affect-processing and thought disorder? *International Journal of Psychoanalysis, 95*(1), 43–66.
Hoffman, L. (2007). Do children get better when we interpret their defenses against painful feelings? *Psychoanalytic Study of the Child, 62*, 291–313.
Holder, A. (2005). *Anna Freud, Melanie Klein, and the psychoanalysis of children and adolescents*. London: Karnac Books.
Kaplan, L. J. (1974). The concept of the family romance. *Psychoanalytic Review, 61*, 169–202.
Klein, M. (1932). *The psycho-analysis of children*. London: Hogarth Press.
Klein, M. (1945). The Oedipus complex in the light of early anxieties. In R. Money-Kyrle (Ed.), *The writings of Melanie Klein* (Vol. 1, pp. 370–419). London: Hogarth Press.
Künstlicher, R. (1996). The function of the frame: To protect the psychoanalytic room. *Scandinavian Psychoanalytic Review, 19*, 150–164.
Laufer, M. (Ed.). (1997). *Adolescent breakdown and beyond*. London: Karnac Books.
Laufer, M., & Laufer, E. M. (1984). *Adolescence and developmental breakdown: A psychoanalytic view*. London: Karnac Books.
Lawrence, M. (2008). *The anorexic mind*. London: Karnac Books.
Lebovici, S. (1982). The origins and development of the Oedipus complex. *International Journal of Psychoanalysis, 63*, 201–215.
Lebovici, S. (2000). La consultation thérapeutique et les interventions métaphorisantes (The therapeutic consultation and the metaphorizing interventions). In M. Maury & M. Lamour (Eds.), *Alliances autour du bébé: De la recherche à la clinique (Alliances around the baby: From research to clinic)* (pp. 223–243). Paris: Presses Universitaires de France.

Leuzinger-Bohleber, M., & Fischmann, T. (2010). Attention-deficit-hyperactivity disorder (AD/HD): A field for contemporary psychoanalysis? Some clinical, conceptual and neurobiological considerations based on the Frankfurt Prevention Study. In J. Tsiantis & J. Trowell (Eds.), *Assessing change in psychoanalytic psychotherapy of children and adolescents: Today's challenge* (pp. 139–176). London: Karnac.

Lieberman, A. F., & Harris, W. W. (2007). Still searching for the best interests of the child: Trauma treatment in infancy and early childhood. *Psychoanalytic Study of the Child, 62*, 211–238.

Lieberman, A. F., & Van Horn, P. (2008). *Psychotherapy with infants and young children: Repairing the effects of stress and trauma on early attachment*. New York, NY: Guilford Press.

Marans, S. (2008). Fear and trauma: Challenges to listening and hearing. *Journal of Infant, Child & Adolescent Psychotherapy, 7*, 165–175.

Murray, L., Arteche, A., Fearon, P., Halligan, S., Croudace, T., & Cooper, P. J. (2010). The effects of maternal postnatal depression and child sex on academic performance at age 16 years: A developmental approach. *Journal of Child Psychology & Psychiatry, 51*(10), 1150–1159.

Murray, L., & Cooper, P. J. (1997). *Postpartum depression and child development*. New York, NY: Guilford Press.

Norman, J. (1991). The analytic frame, theatrical understanding, and interpretation in child analysis. *Scandinavian Psychoanalytic Review, 14*, 139–155.

Norman, J. (2001). The psychoanalyst and the baby: A new look at work with infants. *International Journal of Psychoanalysis, 82*(1), 83–100.

Norman, J. (2004). Transformations of early infantile experiences: A 6-month-old in psychoanalysis. *International Journal of Psychoanalysis, 85*(5), 1103–1122.

O'Shaughnessy, E. (1988a). The invisible Oedipus complex. In E. Bott Spillius (Ed.), *Melanie Klein today: Developments in theory and practice. Vol. 2: Mainly practice* (pp. 191–205). London: Tavistock/Routledge.

O'Shaughnessy, E. (1988b). W. R. Bion's theory of thinking and new techniques in child analysis. In E. Bott Spillius (Ed.), *Melanie Klein today: Developments in theory and practice. Vol. 2: Mainly practice* (pp. 177–190). London: Tavistock/Routledge.

Perret-Catipovic, M., & Ladame, F. (Eds.). (1998). *Adolescence and psychoanalysis: The story and the history*. London: Karnac Books.

Pick, I. B. (1985). Working through in the countertransference. *International Journal of Psychoanalysis, 66*, 157–166.

Racker, H. (1968). *Transference and countertransference*. London: Karnac Books.

Rainwater, J. B. (2007). *A psychoanalytic contribution to the understanding and treatment of attention deficit hyperactivity disorder*. Retrieved from http://gradworks.umi.com/3255212.pdf

Renik, O., Spielman, P., & Afterman, J. (1978). Bamboo phobia in an eighteen-month-old boy. *Journal of the American Psychoanalytic Association, 26*, 255–282.

Ritvo, S. (1996). Observations on the long-term effects of child analysis: Implications for technique. *Psychoanalytic Study of the Child, 51*, 365–385.

Rodriguez, L. R. (1999). *Psychoanalysis with children: History, theory and practice.* London: Free Association Books.

Salomonsson, B. (2004). Some psychoanalytic viewpoints on neuropsychiatric disorders in children. *International Journal of Psychoanalysis, 85*(1), 117–135.

Salomonsson, B. (2006). The impact of words on children with ADHD and DAMP: Consequences for psychoanalytic technique. *International Journal of Psychoanalysis, 87*(4), 1029–1047.

Salomonsson, B. (2007a). Semiotic transformations in psychoanalysis with infants and adults. *International Journal of Psychoanalysis, 88*(5), 1201–1221.

Salomonsson, B. (2007b). "Talk to me baby, tell me what's the matter now": Semiotic and developmental perspectives on communication in psychoanalytic infant treatment. *International Journal of Psychoanalysis, 88*(1), 127–146.

Salomonsson, B. (2011). Psychoanalytic conceptualizations of the internal object in an ADHD child. *Journal of Infant, Child, and Adolescent Psychotherapy, 10*(1), 87–102.

Salomonsson, B. (2012). Has infantile sexuality anything to do with infants? *International Journal of Psychoanalysis, 93*(3), 631–647.

Salomonsson, B. (2014). *Psychoanalytic therapy with infants and parents: Practice, theory and results.* London: Routledge.

Salomonsson, B., & Sandell, R. (2011a). A randomized controlled trial of mother-infant psychoanalytic treatment: 1. Outcomes on self-report questionnaires and external ratings. *Infant Mental Health Journal, 32*(2), 207–231.

Salomonsson, B., & Sandell, R. (2011b). A randomized controlled trial of mother-infant psychoanalytic treatment: 2. Predictive and moderating influences of quantitative treatment and patient factors. *Infant Mental Health Journal, 32*(3), 377–404.

Sandler, J., Kennedy, H., & Tyson, R. (1990). *The technique of child psychoanalysis: Discussions with Anna Freud.* London: Karnac Books.

Solomon, M. (2012). *Beethoven.* London: Schirmer Trade (Kindle edition, Amazon.com).

Sugarman, A. (2006). Attention deficit hyperactivity disorder and trauma. *International Journal of Psychoanalysis, 87*, 237–241.

Tronick, E. (2007). *The neurobehavioral and social-emotional development of infants and children.* New York, NY: Norton.

Tsiantis, J. (Ed.). (2000). *Working with parents of children and adolescents who are in psychoanalytic psychotherapy.* London: Karnac.

Tsiantis, J., Sandler, A.-M., & Martindale, B. (Eds.). (1996). *Countertransference in psychoanalytic psychotherapy with children and adolescents.* London: Karnac Books.

Tyson, R. L. (1978). Notes on the analysis of a prelatency boy with a dog phobia. *Psychoanalytic Study of the Child, 33*, 427–458.

van Buren, J., & Alhanati, S. (Eds.). (2010). *Primitive mental states: A psychoanalytic exploration of the origins of meaning.* London: Routledge.

Waddell, M. (1998). *Inside lives: Psychoanalysis and the growth of personality.* Tavistock Clinic. London: Routledge.

Winberg Salomonsson, M. (1997). Transference in child analysis: A comparative reading of Anna Freud and Melanie Klein. *Scandinavian Psychoanalytic Review, 20*, 1–19.

Winberg Salomonsson, M. (2013). Furious with love: Some reflections on the sexuality of a little girl. In E. Palerm Marí & F. Thomson-Salo (Eds.), *Masculinity and femininity today* (pp. 147–160). London: Karnac.

Winnicott, D. W. (1956/1982). Primary maternal preoccupation. In *Through paediatrics to psycho-analysis* (pp. 300–305). London: Hogarth Press.

Winnicott, D. W. (1971). *Playing and reality*. London: Tavistock.

Zabarenko, L. (2011). ADHD via psychoanalysis, neuroscience, and cognitive psychology: Why haven't we fielded a team? *Journal of Infant, Child & Adolescent Psychotherapy, 10*, 5–12.

Index

ADHD 132, 133, 134, 136; and emotions 133–4; freak 53, 56, 58; treatment 134–5
afraid 17, 18, 33, 67, 74, 85, 98, 99, 100, 113; anger 45, 47, 48, 50, 59, 101; attics 81, 142; Black Man 107–8; the blind 96; boy-girl relationships 30; countertransference 138; crybaby 130; die alone 20; dogs 11; elevator hole 11, 117; feelings 72; ghosts 43, 103, 117, 129; good mother 49; homosexuality 145; life turn into a nightmare 60; mother-daughter relationships 128; parents 140; relationships 32; skulls 44, 45, 46, 47, 48; teenagers and parents 140; volcanoes 72; yourself 105; *see also* fear
"affectionate current" 130
ambivalence 118
analytic frame 120–1, 125
anger 6–7, 21, 22, 23, 24, 27, 28, 29, 30, 31, 32, 33, 40, 41, 45, 46, 47, 48, 50, 51, 52, 56, 59, 62, 64, 72, 76, 77, 92, 101, 103, 104, 105, 107, 120, 121, 122, 128, 129, 130, 131, 133, 137, 140
anxiousness 6, 59, 88–9, 92, 96, 108, 114, 134, 136, 138
attachment theory 129, 130
attention deficit/hyperactivity disorder *see* ADHD

Badoni, M. 120
Beethoven, L. van 117, 119
"beta-elements" 116

Bion, W. R. 9; baby's anxieties 130–1; "beta-elements" 116; "containment" 115; "fear of dying" 131–2; mind 9; "nameless dread" 117; "O" 131; "reverie" 116
black hole 12, 116
Blake, P. 120, 139
Bornstein, B.: "Frankie" 113
Bowlby, J.; attachment 129, 130
bullying 38

calmness 26, 50, 90, 92, 93, 98, 109, 113, 115, 131, 132, 134, 136
Camus, A. 9
central stimulants 134
cognitive help 110
cognitive problems 114
containment 115, 117, 119, 132, 141
control 25, 60, 84, 119, 124; motor 132
countertransference 10, 97, 110, 121–2, 136–7, 138–9
curiosity, 10, 91, 98, 119

DAMP 132
das Unbewußte 8
Daud, A. 136
dead people 43, 48, 129
death 45, 80, 118, 132, 140, 143; brother's 60; grandfather's 142; penalty 85
deficits in attention, motor control and perception *see* DAMP
depression 7; and mother-infant interaction 114–17; postnatal 39, 113–14
det Omedvetna 8, 100

divorce 3, 37, 38, 42, 126; and family romance 126–7
dreams 12, 41–2, 63, 64, 66, 68, 72, 73, 74, 101, 102, 104, 118; letting fantasies loose 125; nasty 20

Ekelöf, G. 9
Emma-will-die 45, 48
emotions 2, 3, 8, 10, 66, 88, 90, 91, 101, 110, 111, 113, 115, 116, 117, 118, 121, 124, 137, 138, 140, 145; ADHD 133–4; problems 97; unconscious 139
evil 89, 90, 91, 92, 117, 119

family romance and divorce 126–7
fantasy 92, 123, 126, 141; and reality 127–9
fear 92, 109, 113, 114, 117, 120, 124, 141, 142, 143; becoming a child again 142; dead people 43, 48, 129; dying 131; mother's 60; parent's 130; sexuality 124; transitory 113; unconscious 130; *see also* afraid
feelings 1, 2, 7, 8, 9, 22, 23, 29, 30, 32, 33–4, 53, 54, 55, 56, 57, 64, 67, 68, 69, 72, 84, 87, 90, 92, 97, 98, 100, 105, 108, 115, 116, 119, 121–2, 125, 130, 131, 133, 134, 137, 138, 141, 144, 145; ambivalent 118; analyst's 136; contradictory 124; creepy 93; exclusion 120, 126; guilt 40, 117; innermost 145; painful 110, 122, 132; strange 142; tingling 75–8, 139–40, 143; toward parents 118; unpleasant 123; warm 83, 84; *see also* anger; emotions; fear; guilt
Field, T. 115
fighting 11, 22–3, 31, 33, 77, 106, 118, 133
first meetings 33, 39, 47, 49, 67, 86–99, 100, 101, 104, 106, 111, 122
Fraiberg, S. 127, 129, 131
Freud, A. 8, 91, 120; adolescent psychoanalysis 145; adolescent will 128; child's play 123
Freud, S.: countertransference 138; *die zärtliche Strömung* (the affectionate current) 130; divided feelings toward parents 118; "the family romance" 126; *The Interpretation of Dreams* 118; "Little Hans" case 113; Oedipus complex 121; sexual drive 130; tragedy of Sophocles 118; transfer representations 137

ghost in the nursery 129–30
Ghost-Mum 101, 103
ghosts 12, 14–16, 17, 43, 51, 89, 91–2, 101–3, 105, 113, 114, 116, 117, 127, 131
Golomb, A. 4
good mother 17, 49
Grotstein, J. 9
guilt 40, 69, 110, 117, 135, 139

harassment 44, 56, 66, 88
hole: black 12, 116; mum- 16–17
hole in the escalator 11–18, 113, 129, 131; black 116; mum- 17–18
homosexuality 145
hyperactivity 6, 133, 134, 136; *see also* ADHD

identity 128, 145; new 143–4
imagination 44, 131, 135, 141; Dickensian 1; lively 37; wild 36
impressions 1, 9, 87–8, 97, 100, 122, 134
impulsivity 133, 134, 135, 136

Klein, M. 91, 120; anxieties 123–4; child's play 123; envy 119; lack of trust 123

"Land of O" 1–2, 5, 6–10, 86, 87, 100, 113, 133, 138, 139; *das Unbewußte* 8; definition 8–9; *det Omedvetna* 8, 100; *Oändligt* 8; Unconscious, 8
Lebovici, S. 119
letter O 1–2, 7–8
liberation 140–1
Lieberman, A. F. 117
Lindgren, Astrid: *Ronia, The Robber's Daughter* 19, 21, 24, 26, 139–40, 141, 143
losing an ability 7
lying 35, 36, 47

Meltzer, D. 91, 145
membrane 9–10
mother-infant interaction and depression 114–17
mother-infant psychoanalysis 4–5, 129, 130–2
mothers, depressed 114, 115, 116
mothers, non-depressed 115
"Mother-will-die" 128
mum-hole 17

nagging 22, 25, 40, 54, 121
negative capability 9
nesting-box 21, 22, 23, 24, 25, 26, 119, 120, 121
neuropsychiatry 97, 98, 132–3
Norman, J. 120, 130–1

Oändligt 8
Oedipus complex 3, 117–19, 121, 122, 124, 140
O'Shaughnessy, E. 116, 118

parents: afraid 140; bonds and liberation 140–1; fear 130; feelings toward 118; teenagers 140; traumatized and their children 135–6
phobias 113, 114
play, meaning of 122–4
postnatal depression 39, 113–14
psychoanalytic frame 96, 119–21
psychoanalytic theory 3–4, 129, 130
psychoanalytic therapy 98, 134
puberty 140

Racker, H. 139
reflections in retrospect 90–2, 109–12
reverie 116
Rodriguez, L. R. 120

sadness 19, 24, 25, 31, 32, 52, 53, 54, 67, 69, 77, 81, 93, 105, 108, 110, 139; mother 16–17, 39–40, 50, 114, 126

Salomonsson, B. 11–18, 21–3, 24–5, 50–2, 53–4, 55–6, 66, 67–9, 70–4, 94, 96, 98, 120–1, 131, 133, 137; mother-infant psychoanalytic treatment 4–5; "Psychoanalytic Therapy with Infants and Parents" 5
Salomonsson, M. Winberg 3, 4, 5, 28–33, 44–8, 88, 92, 93–4, 100–1, 124–5, 129
screaming 39, 41, 49, 50, 52, 87, 115, 131, 139
self-awareness 88
sexual behavior 8, 118, 124, 130, 141; adolescent 143; *see also* homosexuality; Oedipus complex
Sjöberg, B.: "The Songs of Frida" 86
slantwise 51–2
space and freedom 124
Still Face experiment 115

temper 38, 59, 52, 136
tingling feelings 75–8, 139–40, 143
transference 123, 137–8
translation 117, 132
traumatized parents and their children 135–6
traveller's fever 6, 10
Tronick, E. 114–15
Tsiantis, J. 120, 139
typical psychologist response 32–3

Unconscious 3, 8, 9, 10, 87, 100, 115, 130, 138, 139

Van Horn, P. 117
volcano dream 68, 73, 74

weirdness 18, 20, 28, 30–31, 47, 51, 80, 85, 94
why-questions 21, 22
Winnicott, D. W. 116, 140
Wrangsjö, B. 5

"You-will-die" 128